Billy **Graham**

In the footsteps of God's Ambassador

Kevin Belmonte

Day One

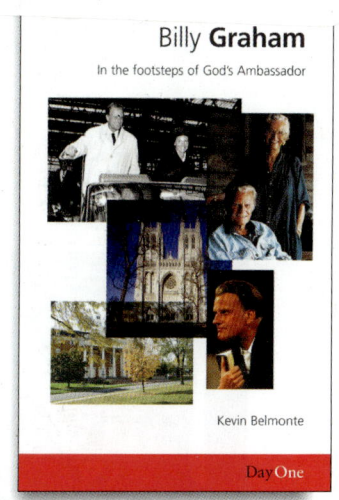

Series Editor: Brian H Edwards

Day One

TRAVEL WITH

Billy **Graham**
In the footsteps of God's Ambassador

The global church

'I have had the privilege of preaching this Gospel on every continent in most of the countries of the world. And I have found that when I present the simple message of the Gospel of Jesus Christ…He takes the message and drives it supernaturally into the human heart'

A hallmark of Billy Graham's ministry in the 1970s was The International Congress on World Evangelization, held at Lausanne, Switzerland in July 1974, or, as it came to be more familiarly known, 'Lausanne '74.' He and his colleagues in the BGEA were very aware of the good that had been done for the spread of the gospel internationally as The World Congress on Evangelism held in Berlin, West Germany from October 25 through November 4, 1966. There was an important spiritual pedigree for both events. The archives of The Billy Graham Center at Wheaton College reveal that The Berlin Congress was 'intended as a spiritual successor of the 1910 World Missionary Conference in Edinburgh, Scotland.' The watchword for the Edinburgh Conference had been 'the evangelization of the world in this generation.' Both the Berlin and Lausanne events wished to carry that watchword and that commitment forward.

The theme of the Lausanne Congress, attended by over 4,000 evangelical leaders from some 150 countries, was 'Let the earth hear His voice.' Held in the Palais de Beaulieu, its intention was to begin the process of dialogue

Facing page: Billy Graham, solemnly committed to the power of prayer.

Right: A session from Lausanne '74, the profoundly influential congress on world evangelism convened by Billy Graham, John Stott and other Christian leaders of international renown.

Ambassador for Christ

'All that I had been able to do I owe to Jesus Christ. When you honor me you are really honoring him. Any honors I have received I accept with a sense of inadequacy and humility and I will reserve the right to hand all of these someday to Christ, when I see him face-to-face'

In anything, the international scene dominated the 1980s more than it had the 1970s. Far-sweeping changes were in the air. Billy Graham was close to the epicenter of many key events, including the dawn of the post-communist world. In 1981, much of the world was still caught up in what had come to be called The Cold War. For America, Britain and the Soviet Union, it was the era of détente. Meanwhile, hard economic times were a reality for many in the United States. The final months of Jimmy Carter's presidency were overshadowed by these realities, as they were by the seemingly insoluble hostage crisis in Iran. Billy Graham extended a hand of friendship to President Carter during his administration, as he did to Carter's successor Ronald Reagan. Tragedy very nearly ended Reagan's presidency before it was six months old. An assassin's bullet almost claimed the new President's life on 30 March 1981. For many who watched that awful event unfold on television and prayed the president would survive, it seemed as though a deeply troubled world had suddenly become a darker place still.

To Russia, with love
It was a trying time. And yet, as so often is the case, the most difficult times can be times when God strikes a way where there had been none before. It was just a little over a year after the attempt on President Reagan's life, and not long after a series of crusades in New England, that God opened the door for Billy Graham to go to Russia. As envisioned, this visit would be relatively brief, lasting for a week, from 7–13 May 1982. The prospect was met with no little amount of controversy. America's

Facing page: Preaching in East Germany from Martin Luther's pulpit.

Right: Billy Graham, with Ronald and Nancy Reagan at the 1989 Anaheim Crusade.

CONTENTS

- Meet Billy Graham **5** 
  1. A son of the south **7**
  2. An unforeseen course **21**
  3. A story to tell to the nations **37** 
  4. New opportunities—troubled horizons **53**
  5. The global church **67**
  6. Ambassador for Christ **79** 
  7. Passing the mantle **93**
  8. The lasting legacy **107**
- An epilogue from Billy Graham **118**
- A time line for Billy Graham **120** 
- Further reading and books by Billy **122**
- Acknowledgements and Author **123**
- Further books in this series **124-127** 
- A map of Billy's UK crusades **128**
- A map of Billy's world crusades: **inside front cover**

© Day One Publications 2010   First printed 2010

A CIP record is held at The British Library   ISBN 978-1-84625-156-6

Published by Day One Publications Ryelands Road, Leominster, HR6 8NZ

℡ 01568 613 740 FAX 01568 611 473 email: sales@dayone.co.uk   www.dayone.co.uk   All rights reserved

No part of this publication may be reproduced, or stored in a retrieval system, or transmitted, in any form or by any means, mechanical, electronic, photocopying, recording or otherwise, without the prior permission of Day One Publications

Design: studiohope limited, www.studiohope.co.uk   Printed by Polskabook, UK

Dedication: To Ken Hayes and Brian Edwards, friends who have shown me many kindnesses, not least the gift of their friendship.

Meet Billy Graham

To say 'meet Billy Graham' seems almost unnecessary. Few people, either in Britain, America, or throughout the rest of the world, are so widely known. Since the 1940s, Dr. Graham has preached to nearly 215 million people. Over 185 countries and territories have borne witness to his faithful stewardship of the Great Commission. He has been a valued friend to presidents, and leaders of every description. In December 2001 he was given an honorary knighthood by Queen Elizabeth II for his international contribution to civic and religious life. The world had truly become his parish.

But it was not always so. Raised on a farm in North Carolina, amidst the hardships of the Great Depression, few would have predicted the future for Graham that followed. Everything changed in 1934 when, at the age of sixteen, he made a decision for Christ on the proverbial 'sawdust trail'. That decision has since led to the spiritual transformation of millions of lives.

For over fifty years, Dr. Graham's ministry has been international in scope. It all started in London's Harringay Arena in the spring of 1954. Two million people attended crusades over a period of three months, and thousands came to faith. Sir Winston Churchill met with Dr. Graham, and he was invited to preach before Queen Elizabeth in the chapel of Windsor Castle. The Harringay Crusade opened the door for scores of subsequent crusades throughout the world. Through all of the intervening years—whether in Asia, Africa, South America or Europe, in nations of the Pacific rim or those whose shores are met by the waters of the Atlantic—Dr. Graham's message has remained the same: 'My one purpose… is to help people find a personal relationship with God, which, I believe, comes through knowing Christ.'

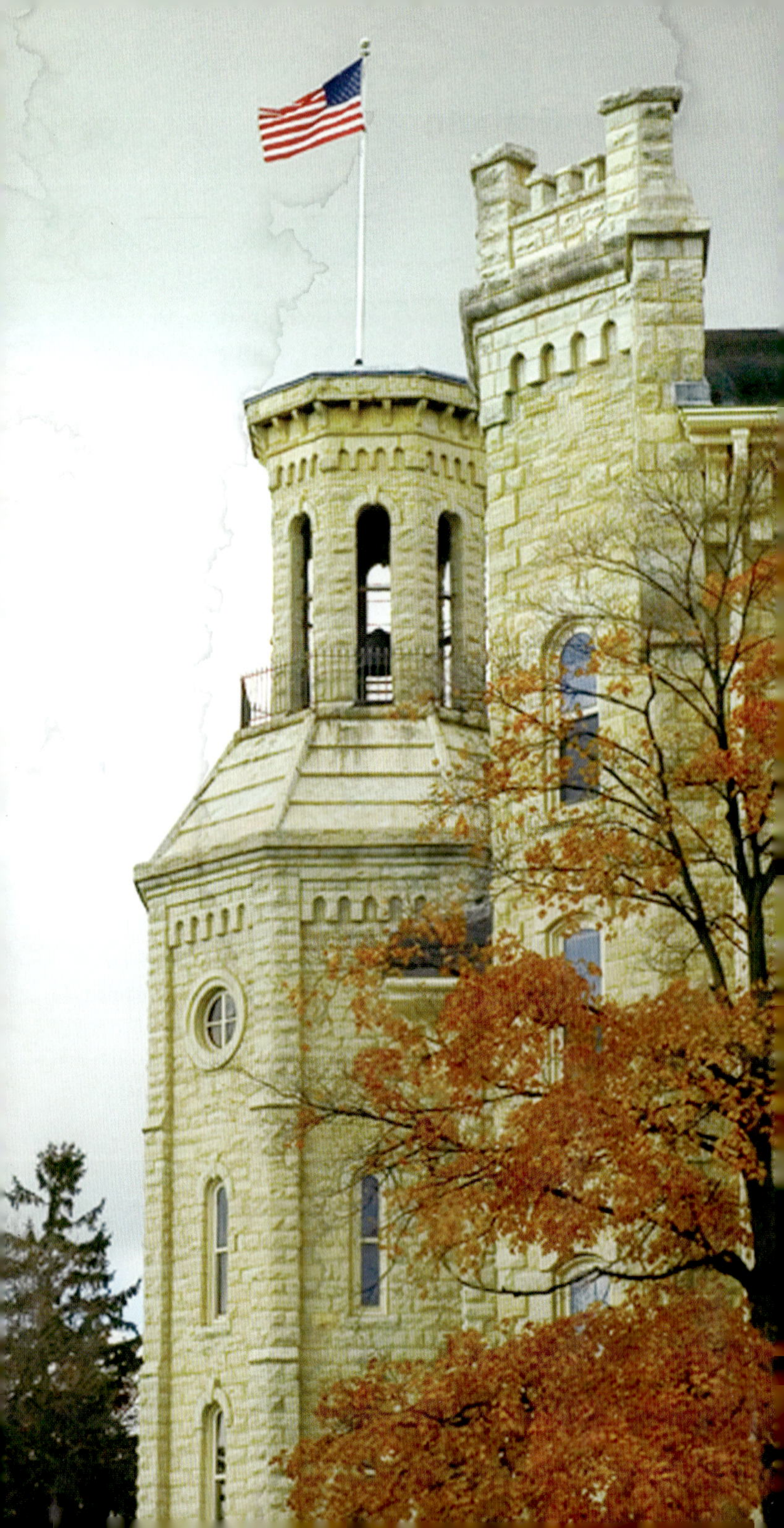

1 A son of the South

'When my decision for Christ was made, I walked slowly down and knelt in prayer. I opened my heart and knew for the first time the sweetness and joy of God, of truly being born again... I knew in my heart that I was somehow different and changed. That night absolutely changed the direction of my life'

When Billy Graham was born in a frame farmhouse outside Charlotte, North Carolina, on 7 November 1918, World War I had not yet ended. Americans still fought in what many people hoped was 'the war to end all wars'. America herself was little more than fifty years removed from the Civil War, a conflict in which Graham's maternal and paternal grandfathers had fought. An agricultural way of life was still common, and industrialization had yet to reach many parts of the United States.

The world into which Billy Graham was born was very different from our own. He learned what it was to work on the family dairy farm, and how those responsibilities shaped the cycle of each day. While still in elementary school, he also came to understand that his family was heir to a legacy of faith. Some years before Billy was born, his maternal grandfather Ben Coffey had died. A brave soldier, he had been blinded in one eye and had his left leg amputated, but throughout his life he had been a man of faith. As a boy, Billy had known his maternal grandmother Lucinda, and on her deathbed those gathered by her witnessed a remarkable scene: Just before her passing, she sat up, and in a voice that seemed most like laughter, exclaimed: 'I see Jesus. He has his arms outstretched toward me.

Above: Billy Graham, at six months, with his mother

Facing page: Blanchard Tower at Wheaton College where Billy Graham met Ruth McCue Bell during their student days

Above: A Civil War scene from the Battle of Chickamauga, fought from 19–20 September 1863, during which the forces of the Union suffered a crushing defeat at the hands of the Confederacy

And there's Ben. He has both of his eyes and both of his legs.'

In the early 1930s, the Great Depression enveloped America. The Grahams were fortunate, because as farmers they were able to live off the land. Nevertheless, it was a time of widespread poverty and, surrounded by his extended family, Billy saw how they supported each other. A thoughtful and active child, he relished play with family pets, among them a collie, and developed a lifelong fondness for walks alone in the countryside. He grew to love baseball, becoming a capable fielder, though something of an unorthodox hitter, batting cross-handed from the left side of home plate. However, baseball provided a connection of another sort. When Billy was five, his father had taken him to hear the popular baseball player turned preacher, Billy Sunday. The event made no lasting impression on the young boy, but it was of a piece with the Christian atmosphere Billy's parents tried to create in their home.

Always, there were times set apart each day for what Billy Graham's mother called 'the family altar'. The Grahams would seek 'heavenly help to keep the family together.' Billy never forgot these occasions, and years later reflected: 'Every time my mother prayed with one of us, and every time my parents prayed for their sons and daughters, they were declaring their dependence on God for the wisdom and strength and courage to stay in control of life, no matter what circumstances might bring. Beyond that, they prayed for their children, that they might come into the kingdom of God.' Billy's family had need of such strength as prayer and the teachings God's word could give. In 1932 his father nearly died in a freak accident when he was struck in the mouth with great force by a piece of wood thrown free of a mechanical saw. Rushed to a nearby hospital, it was not known for days if he would live. Billy's mother asked everyone she knew to pray, and slowly the danger passed. Skilled surgeons reconstructed his father's face, and in time he fully recovered. Ever

Above: The 'homeplace' where Billy Graham was raised

Billy Sunday — 'the fastest man in baseball'

William Ashley Sunday (1862–1935) was for many years a professional baseball player, his great speed making him a skilled base runner and outfielder. Before his playing days ended, 'Billy' was converted to faith in Christ, and eventually left baseball to work in a Chicago YMCA. In time, he became an assistant to J. Wilber Chapman, a popular evangelist in the early 1890s. Sunday eventually formed his own ministry, where his athleticism was much in evidence. Before his meetings, held under large tents or specially constructed wooden 'tabernacles', he would often play in exhibition games. His prowess, and energetic, vibrant preaching drew audiences of increasing size. At times he might pretend to slide into home plate, as a baseball player would, or brandish a wooden chair, bringing it down hard upon the platform. Such theatrics were his way of making a point. His was a muscular form of Christianity. It was popular as well. Sunday preached to over 100 million people, and a conservative estimate holds that one million people were converted through his ministry, though the number is likely to have been far higher. Increasingly influential, Billy offered an opening prayer for the US House of Representatives in 1908, and was on separate occasions asked to dine with Presidents Theodore Roosevelt and Woodrow Wilson. The multimillionaire John D. Rockefeller was deeply appreciative of Sunday's work, and sponsored his crusades for years on the condition of anonymity. Sunday died of a sudden heart attack on 6 November 1935. Tens of thousands of mourners filed past his casket in the Moody Memorial Church in Chicago.

Above left: Billy Sunday during his playing days

Above right: Billy Sunday, making an energetic pose during a sermon, circa 1914

Far left:
Billy Graham's parents, Frank and Morrow Graham

Left: Billy Graham, age seven, with his father and sister Catherine

after, his parents believed that God had graciously intervened.

Billy was deeply grateful for his father's recovery, but in the years that followed, other concerns came to dominate his life. Although he respected his parents' beliefs, by his teenage years Billy cared little for matters of faith. This became clear when the Rev. Mordecai Ham arrived for a series of preaching crusades in and around the Charlotte area in 1935. Billy had just turned sixteen, an age when many young people question their parents or their parents' interests. He wanted nothing to do with an evangelist like Ham and told his parents he wouldn't go to hear him. Or so he thought. For a month Billy resisted all attempts to get him to go to Ham's meetings; evangelistic crusades then went on for weeks

The sawdust trail

The phrase 'the sawdust trail' has entered American speech for someone taking a route towards their rehabilitation. However, it originated from the evangelistic meetings of Billy Sunday in the early 20th century. Most of his meetings were held in temporary wooden buildings, often referred to as 'tabernacles', into which people packed sitting on hard wooden chairs or benches. The floor of the aisle was strewn with sawdust to soften the sound of hundreds of feet on the bare boards. The journey down the aisle to the platform at the front as a mark of repentance and acceptance of Christ became known as 'the sawdust trail'. The enquirer would shake the hand of the evangelist before being passed on to a counsellor. The phrase became synonymous with 'conversion'. Later, the preaching circuit of an evangelist was itself known as 'the sawdust trail'. The phrase became the butt of jokes for the sceptics but it had a serious meaning for those whose lives were transformed by their response to Christ. The extensive and careful planning of Billy Sunday's campaigns clearly influenced the detailed preparation for Billy Graham's crusades in later years. Sunday used a small team of co-workers, including his wife Helen often known simply as Ma. They took charge of the business and advertising side, prayer groups, music, counselling and follow-up. Clergy from the local churches, as well as lay volunteers, were used as much as possible. A pamphlet was produced to advise those who were enlisted to counsel those who walked the trail. Billy Sunday held his first campaign in Garner, Iowa in 1896 and continued preaching for the next half-century -- an example that Billy Graham also followed!

at a time. But no matter how long Ham stayed, Billy was determined to stay away.

However, one night he finally agreed to attend when a friend told him that if he did he would hear a *fighting* preacher. Curiosity drew him. He would see for himself if Ham was the fighter he was said to be. When Ham began to speak, Billy realized he had never heard a sermon like this. Returning home, he lay awake in his bed for a long time, thinking. He went back the next night, and the next. Those nights became a week and one week became two. Ham spoke about the wages of sin, and hell as a place of eternal torment. But he also spoke of God's love. Stranger still, Ham had a fine sense of wit, and he could tell stories almost as well as Billy's father could. But Ham's pulpit oratory notwithstanding, it was one verse of Scripture that proved the climax of the inner struggle Billy was experiencing about the need to have a personal relationship with Christ and seek forgiveness for his sins. It was 'a gentle reminder,' Billy recalled, that touched him most, a verse from the Book of Romans: 'But God,' Ham declared, 'commendeth his love for us, in that, while we were yet sinners, Christ died for us.' The choir then sang 'Just as I am', followed by 'Almost persuaded, now to believe'. At the last verse of 'Almost persuaded' Billy walked down the sawdust-strewn aisle to stand before the platform. He was met by a family friend who explained the way of salvation, and what it meant to be a genuine

Above: *Interior of 'The Tabernacle' at Scranton, Pennsylvania; a typical evangelistic setting where sawdust was used to cover the floor to deaden unnecessary sound—hence the expression 'The sawdust trail'*
Inset: *Evangelist Mordecai Ham, faithful herald of 'the sawdust trail'*

Christian. The man prayed, and guided Billy in a prayer of his own. When it was over Billy Graham, the teenage rebel, felt as though he had made a real commitment to Christ. He cried no tears, nor did he feel the rush of emotion he saw in others that night. His was a quiet understanding: 'I simply felt at peace,' he remembered. 'Quiet, not delirious. Happy and peaceful.'

The college student

Gradually, in little ways, those around Billy began to notice that something was different. His mother remembered that he grew more thoughtful and kind. These things caught the eye of his high school principal, Mr. Hutchinson. But for the most part, Billy's transformation took place deep within, and in ways he scarcely understood. He was seemingly far removed from any public declarations of his new found faith—but that was about to change. Early in 1936, when Billy was seventeen, a preacher named Jimmie Johnson took him to an evangelistic service at a nearby jail. As Johnson spoke, Billy watched, as much a spectator as any inmate present. Then, halfway through his sermon, Johnson pointed to Billy and said, 'Here's a young fellow who can tell you what it's like to be converted.' Stunned, Billy somehow managed to get to his feet and utter 'three or four sentences' before sitting down again. It was not an auspicious beginning, but it was at least a beginning.

In the months that followed, Billy occasionally gave his testimony, along with other friends who were members of a Bible club. He was anything but a commanding presence. His friend Grady Wilson remembered Billy as 'scattered and rattling. He'd just stand there and twist his coat very nervously. He appeared awfully shy and timid.' He was still very much finding his way, which was underscored by the fact that it was his mother who decided where he would go to college. Billy entered Bob Jones College in Cleveland, Tennessee, in the summer of 1936. But he didn't stay long. As the distinguished biographer John Pollock has written: 'Billy needed careful handling if latent intellectual and spiritual powers were to be drawn out. But Bob Jones College ran in fixed grooves. 'Dr. Bob' knew exactly what was true and false in faith, ethics and academics, and often stated publicly that his institution had never been wrong. Independent thought was so discouraged that many alumni later said there was almost thought control. All this,

Above: Billy Graham, about the time he came to faith in 1935

Above: The Florida Bible Institute, where Billy Graham commenced his studies in 1937

together with a bout of 'flu, made Billy reluctant to return to Bob Jones College after Christmas.' Mrs. Graham put her finger on the trouble: 'It was not so much the studies as the all-round strenuous schedule put in practice there from early morning until late at night which will sometimes detract very greatly from the deepening of spiritual things.' She wanted a 'quiet, spiritual atmosphere for Billy.'

Billy's departure from Bob Jones College was difficult. The idea that anyone would leave his school rankled Jones. 'Billy,' he said, 'if you leave and throw your life away at a little country Bible School, the chances are you'll never be heard of. At the best, all you could amount to would be a poor country Baptist preacher somewhere out in the sticks.'

In January 1937 Billy and his parents arrived on the campus of the Florida Bible Institute at Temple Terrace, near Tampa. Here Billy would spend what he later called 'three and one half glorious, happy, character building, life changing years.' The school was neither a liberal arts college nor a seminary, but its students received a thorough grounding in the English Bible, with courses in related subjects: Greek, church history and missions, hermeneutics and pastoral theology, as well as practical training in Christian service. Most importantly, students were not subjected to a rigid intellectual system. They were encouraged to think, while teachers sought to cultivate their individual talents. The guiding principle was that 'the Holy Spirit, if allowed to operate in His own time and way, could make of a man what He would.'

Billy's time at the Florida Bible Institute was happy in many ways, but not altogether. In 1938, he fell in love with and become engaged to a fellow student named Emily Cavanaugh. But after much soul-searching, Emily told him her heart really belonged to another. It was a painful episode and a time of great uncertainty. However, one thing emerged from Billy's time at the Institute: he felt sure that God had called him to be a preacher. His first opportunity to preach came unexpectedly. One of his tutors at the Institute asked him to accompany him to Bostwick Baptist Church in Florida, and on the journey announced that Billy would be preaching. His protests were overruled with the assurance 'When you run out, I'll take over.' Billy had learnt four sermons by heart, each scheduled to last for forty minutes. In the event he ran through all four in less than ten minutes!

In 1939, while he was still attending the Florida Bible Institute, Billy was ordained within the Southern Baptist denomination. When he graduated in 1940, he had been given a fine foundation upon which to build, having been mentored by caring teachers and thoroughly trained in the Scriptures. However, it was clear that while his early efforts at preaching were earnest, they were also rough around the edges. Those who listened to Billy preach sensed his potential, but felt he needed further training and guidance. One of those who heard him was Elner Edman, whose brother Ray was interim president at Wheaton; another was Paul Fischer, whose brother Herman was chairman of the board there. They made Billy an astounding offer: Fischer would pay for Billy's first year of tuition at Wheaton, while Edman would agree to help with other expenses. Solid references and funds were what Billy needed. With such generous support, he applied for admission and was accepted. It was a remarkable turn of events.

College in the Midwest

Wheaton College was the answer to his mother's prayers. Billy later learned that for four years she had been praying he would go there. She had met its former president, James Oliver Buswell, and had been deeply impressed. This meeting planted the seeds of a cherished hope, and now those seeds, watered with faithful, secret prayer, had borne fruit.
Billy arrived at Wheaton feeling

Left: Billy Graham in 1937, with two of his instructors from the Florida Bible Institute, John Minder and Cecil Underwood

somewhat out of place. He was older than most students and from a farming country in the south, whilst Wheaton, in Illinois, was in the suburban midwest. With its handsome buildings and well-tended grounds, it was cosmopolitan compared with what he knew. Certainly he had received tremendous encouragement from men prominently associated with the school, but had he made a mistake? Billy's early misgivings were laid to rest when he met Dr. Mortimer B. Lane and his family. Professor of government

Above: *The Billy Graham Center at Wheaton College*

Wheaton— 'the Harvard of evangelical colleges'

Founded in 1860, Wheaton College is a top-ranked, academically rigorous Christian liberal arts college located west of Chicago, Illinois. It is home to an internationally recognized Conservatory of Music and distinguished Graduate School. Undergraduate students may choose from forty majors in the liberal arts disciplines and sciences. Wheaton is also the site of the prestigious Marion R. Wade Center, established by Professor of English Clyde S. Kilby in 1965 as an extensive research library and museum of the books and papers of seven British writers: C.S. Lewis, G.K. Chesterton, J.R.R. Tolkien, Owen Barfield, Dorothy L. Sayers, George MacDonald and Charles Williams. The Wade Center also houses other possessions once owned by these writers, including the wardrobe made by C.S. Lewis' grandfather (made famous in *The Chronicles of Narnia* books) and the writing desk at which J.R.R. Tolkien wrote *The Hobbit* and worked on *The Lord of the Rings*. Other prominent writers who have donated their papers to Wheaton include Pulitzer Prize nominee Frederick Buechner and Madeline L'Engle, winner of the Newbury Medal for her book *A Wrinkle in Time*.

Wheaton is the site of The Billy Graham Center. Established in 1980, the BGC houses the corporate records for the Billy Graham Evangelistic Association, several evangelism institutes, a museum of the history of evangelism and Wheaton College's Archives and Special Collections. Wheaton's motto is *Christo et Regno Ejus* (For Christ and His Kingdom).

Above: *Blanchard Tower at Wheaton College shrouded in a Christmas snow*

and economics, Dr. and Mrs. Lane, along with their seven children, lived in a large Victorian home near the Wheaton campus. Billy became one of the family, and in an atmosphere of kindness and understanding he began to thrive. Looking back on his college years, he reflected: 'Wheaton was both a spiritual and an intellectual turning point in my life.'

A life partner

Wheaton was also the setting in which Billy Graham met his wife, Ruth. She would become, as he later claimed, his 'life partner'— they were together for sixty-three years. In fact, they could not have been more different. Both had a deep love for Christ, but their upbringings were worlds apart: Billy was a son of the American south from a rural environment largely protected from the harsh world around, whereas Ruth had been born in China to medical missionary parents. It was there she spent the first seventeen years of her life, and some aspects of her early life were harrowing.

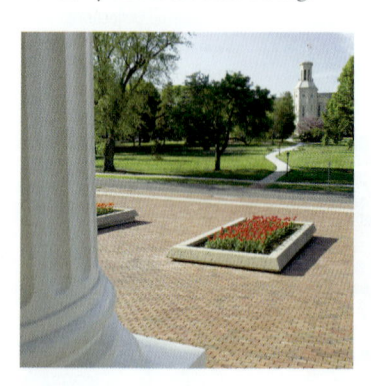

Above: *A view of Blanchard Tower from the pillared steps of The Billy Graham Center at Wheaton College*

Living in a hospital compound with her family in the eastern Chinese province of Northern Kiangsu, Ruth had first hand experience of bandit attacks and civil war. Her education was international in scope, as she attended the Foreign School in Pyongyang in North Korea.

A friend had pointed out Ruth to Billy during his first term at Wheaton, but it had taken him a month to summon the courage to ask her out on a date. Together they attended a performance of Handel's *Messiah* in Wheaton's Pierce Chapel. After the performance, they shared a cup of tea and talked for a long time. Billy, like so many of his classmates, thought Ruth beautiful, witty and talented; but he was also deeply impressed with her love for Christ and her desire to serve him. Billy had also made a deep impression, but he did not know he had until Ruth told him about it some time later. That evening she returned to her room, knelt and prayed, telling God that if she could spend the rest of her life serving him with Billy, 'she would consider it the greatest privilege imaginable.' They had both fallen quickly and deeply in love.

In the weeks to come, Billy and Ruth continued to see one another, treasuring those moments when they could be together. But, Billy later remembered, it was not long before 'one minor problem kept coming up.' Ruth felt a deep conviction that God had called her to missionary service in Tibet. What is more, she wanted Billy to go with her. Billy, for his part, felt

Right: The entrance to Wheaton College

certain that God had called him to be a gospel preacher at home. He was not averse to serving God in Tibet; but it was a prospect very different from anything on which he had bargained. Ruth's determination to follow God's call was so pronounced that she told Billy about Mildred Cable, a missionary who had rejected a young man she loved because marriage would have precluded her going to China. The two young people were torn. Billy remembered that during this time of uncertainty there were only two things he was sure of: that Ruth would marry someday, and that he was the one she would marry. But how would this come about? It was only natural for him to try to persuade her as his heart led, but in spite of their many discussions, they could not seem to agree on this vital issue.

There were other points of difference as well. Ruth had a Presbyterian upbringing, while Billy was an ordained Baptist minister. In the way that countless young people have experienced, each felt an allegiance to the faith tradition of their youth. Both had strong wills; but over time each began to learn that they weren't so very far apart in the things that mattered most, and that adjustments in their thinking were not impossible. Progress on this front was encouraging, but after Billy proposed marriage in the summer of 1941, Ruth found herself in the midst of a serious struggle once more. She believed God had brought them together, but despite her request that he remain open to the idea of service on the mission field, she felt a growing realization that God was not leading him in that direction.

The turning point came in the middle of Billy's second semester at Wheaton when Ruth left school to care for her sister Rosa in New Mexico, who had been diagnosed with tuberculosis. Meanwhile, after school let him out for a series of summer preaching engagements, Billy had returned to the south. The young couple wrote letters and continued to pray that God would guide them as to their future. Billy's world changed forever when he received a letter Ruth had written on 6 July 1941. It contained three words he had been longing to hear: 'I'll marry you.' All the while they had been apart, she felt God had been working in her heart, helping her to reach

Far left: Billy Graham and Ruth McCue Bell, newly engaged

Left: Billy and Ruth Graham on their wedding day

a decision. Billy confesses that that same evening he was due to preach, but he was so ecstatic that he could think of little else than the letter. At the close of the sermon the pastor asked him 'Do you know what you just said?' Billy replied 'No'. To which the pastor responded, 'I'm not sure the people did either.'

Overjoyed, Billy went out straightaway and bought an engagement ring, and at the earliest opportunity he drove to where Ruth was staying. They had a tender reunion, and he gave her the ring. Ruth was deeply moved, but told him apologetically that she could not wear the ring until she had her parents' consent. A telegram was immediately sent, followed by what seemed to the impatient couple an interminable waiting. Ruth's message had been short and to the point: 'Bill has offered me a ring. May I wear it?' At last the equally brief reply came back: 'Yes—if it fits.'

Shortly after, Ruth's sister Rosa recovered and Ruth was able to return to Wheaton. But there were still some anxious moments, and for a time Ruth felt serious doubts about the prospect of marriage. They centered on Billy's convictions about service on the mission field. It just wasn't where he felt God was leading him. Ruth's doubts were such that she felt they ought to cease dating. When Billy responded that in that case it would be best for her to return his ring, she refused! Ruth had become deeply attached to it, and this realization, it seems, is what finally resolved her doubts. It had at times been difficult. Theirs was a hard-won, yet no less cherished belief that God

Above: The Graham family 'homeplace'—the childhood home of Billy Graham, North Carolina

had brought them together. Two months after their graduation from Wheaton in June 1943, on Friday 13 August, William Franklin Graham and Ruth McCue Bell were married in the idyllic setting of Montreat, a Presbyterian conference center in the mountains of North Carolina where Ruth's parents had made their home.

Theirs was to be a marriage well suited for the work to which God had called them. Years later, and looking back over a lifetime of worldwide ministry, Billy offered this following tribute to his wife: 'Ruth and I were called by God as a team. She urged me to go, saying, "God has given you the gift of an evangelist. I'll back you. I'll rear the children and you travel and preach."… I'd come home and she had everything so organized and so calmed down that they all seemed to love me. But that was because she taught them to.'

TRAVEL INFORMATION

The Billy Graham Library

The Billy Graham Library 4330 Westmont Drive in Charlotte, North Carolina. www.billygraham.org/BGLibrary
Visitors can tour the restored Graham Family home, where they can explore the life and legacy of Billy Graham's dearly loved wife in a special room dedicated to Ruth Bell Graham, or spend time in prayer and reflection in the library's Prayer Garden.

As the library website states, its centerpiece exhibit is *A Journey of Faith*, a presentation that features multimedia displays and re-creations of historic moments in Billy Graham's life and ministry. Spanning the decades from the 1940s to the present, the exhibits show how God prepared and used this humble man to take the message of God's unchanging love to an ever-changing world. Visitors should note that groups of 15 or more require a reservation. The library staff requests that such groups e-mail in advance at librarytours@bgea.org or call ahead on 704–401–3200. The library is closed on Sundays. Admission is free of charge.

The Billy Graham Center

Wheaton College in Illinois
Essential to explore all facets of the life and legacy of Billy Graham and the Billy Graham Evangelistic Association (BGEA). Departments within this one-of-a-kind facility include the BGC Museum, an Institute of Strategic Evangelism, and an Institute for Cross-Cultural Training.

The homepage for the Billy Graham Center is: www.billygrahamcenter.com

Those planning a visit to the center may email in advance at BGCADM@wheaton.edu or call 630–752–5157.

Not to be missed when visiting Wheaton College is The Wade Center, the world-class repository of all things relating to the Inklings, the group of writers associated with C.S. Lewis and J.R.R. Tolkien.

To visit the Wade Center's homepage, go to: www.wheaton.edu/wadecenter

For a complete set of travel directions by air and by car travel, go to: www.wheaton.edu/wadecenter/welcome/visitor_info.html

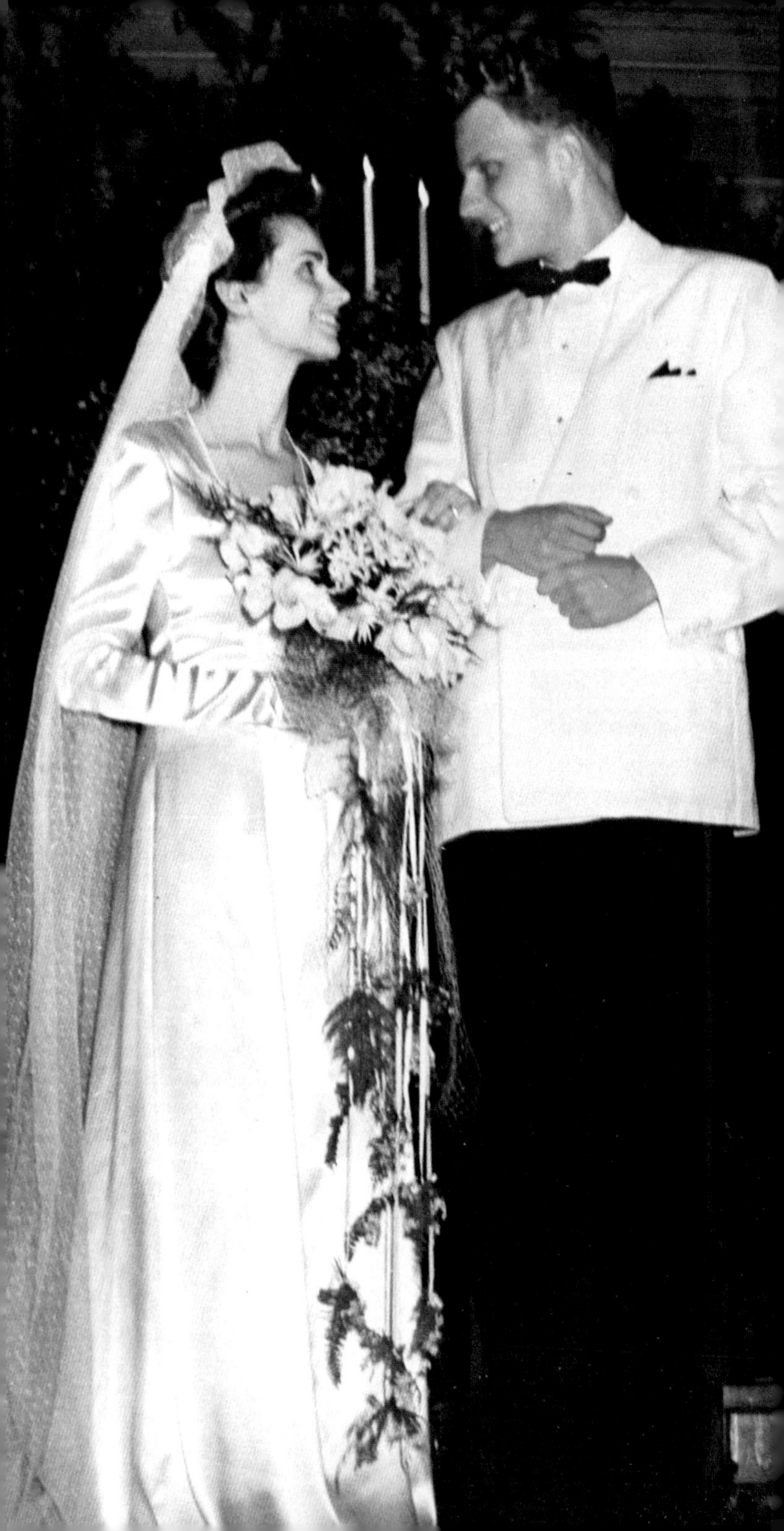

❷ An unforeseen course

'I read Ephesians again and again, where it mentions that the Lord gave some to be evangelists and some to be pastors. God just did not want me to be a pastor. It was time to take up what the Lord called me to do—evangelism'

Following their marriage, Billy Graham's life started down a predictable path. He accepted a call to pastor a Baptist church in Western Springs, a semi-rural, affluent suburb of Chicago. This might well have been welcome news to Ruth, but Billy had accepted this call, promising though it may have been, without consulting her. She was understandably angry over this, since she believed that life-changing decisions were things to be agreed upon through mutual discussion and prayer. Sincerely apologetic, Billy had learned a valuable lesson.

The little church was indeed modest, so small that it met in the basement of what its fewer than one hundred members hoped might in time become a church building; Ruth wryly observed that it was rather like meeting in an air-raid shelter. However, the 'Village Church', as it came to be called, had a hunger to see what God would do, and that counted for much. Over time, the little church began to thrive. Billy preached twice on Sundays and attended youth meetings in members' homes. Ruth, a partner in ministry, taught child evangelism classes and went with Billy on many pastoral calls. All the while, he looked ahead to an eventual Army Chaplaincy, which he hoped to pursue in earnest after a year of pastoral ministry.

At the same time, Billy accepted offers to speak in other towns, and these began to increase steadily. Much of the reason appeared to stem from Billy's willingness to think outside the box when it came to ministry opportunities. True enough, he did as other

Above: *In the darkest days of the blitz, Britain's courage never faltered*

Facing page: *Billy and Ruth Graham on their wedding day*

new ministers did, visiting local residents who had no church affiliation, but he also began to seek out population groups not previously evangelized—storekeepers in particular—some of whom other ministers had preferred not to be seen with. Billy longed to tell anyone who would listen about Christ, and he took seriously the command to 'go into all the world and preach the gospel to every creature' (Mark 16:15 NKJV). He did not for one minute believe this command had

Above: *The type of radio to which families would listen to hear broadcasts of* Songs in the Night

been rescinded, nor did he think it applied solely to missionaries, as some Christians had deluded themselves into thinking. If Christ sought out 'tax collectors and sinners' and cared deeply for them, Billy Graham could do no less.

Because Billy wanted to reach out to all sections of society, he worked with his chairman of the deacons, Bob Van Kampen, to start the Western Suburban Professional Men's Club. The club met for dinner several times during the winter months, followed by an evangelistic talk. But Billy didn't wait for word of mouth to swell the club's ranks. He sought individual meetings with prominent businessmen. Despite tight schedules and any reservations they may have had, they detected something winsome and genuine about this young man. Many were persuaded, and in time more than three hundred men were attending the dinners.

On the air

Word began to spread about the Village Church and its young preacher, which led to Billy receiving a phone call in October 1943 that changed the course of his life and ministry. The Rev. Torrey Johnson, then a popular religious broadcaster in the greater Chicago area, wanted to know if Billy and the Village Church would assume responsibility for one of his programs called *Songs in the Night*. Carried live by one of the city's most widely heard radio stations, the program typically consisted of 45 minutes of preaching and singing. It aired at 10:15 every Sunday morning. This was a tremendous opportunity—but there was a catch. A one hundred dollar a week fee was required by the radio station and they were asking that Billy and the Village Church commit to a contract of thirteen weeks. The income of the church was only $86.50 per week, so a decision to move forward would require a tremendous venture of faith in order to blaze a new trail of ministry. The deacons with whom Billy served felt overwhelmed by it all. But as one of them later

Right: George Beverly Shea, Billy Graham's great friend, and the featured soloist for the Songs in the Night *radio program*

recalled, Billy 'had the gift of getting people to respond in faith.' Within three months, enough money had been raised to cover the first five broadcasts.

But how to structure the program? Billy envisioned something special, and so he decided to approach the prominent soloist George Beverly Shea about becoming the featured musician for *Songs in the Night*. Billy did not know Shea, nor had he secured a means of introduction. He simply drove to the headquarters of WMBI, the flagship radio station of the Moody Bible Institute, and asked to see the singer who also served as a WMBI program manager and announcer. Politely rebuffed by an office receptionist, Billy turned to leave, and then thought, 'No, I've come to see him. I'm going to see him.' He stepped purposefully by the receptionist's desk and walked into Shea's office. It was a fateful, if unorthodox meeting. Billy, it seemed, could persuade others besides his church members to respond in faith. *Songs in the Night*, featuring George Beverly Shea, first aired in January 1944.

The Lord rewarded the faith of both Graham and Shea, and the members of the Village Church. Substantial funds to support this new ministry soon began to come in, and it was a happy day when Billy burned the church mortgage in a pie plate as happy church members looked on. As designed by Billy and Ruth Graham and George Beverly Shea, *Songs in the Night* was innovative. Ruth helped write the scripts, which presented an overview of recent news and world events that set the stage for a compelling declaration of the gospel. Listeners, especially young people, responded warmly to this format. It allowed Billy to present the timeless truths of the gospel in a manner relevant to their concerns. Shea's rich baritone voice attracted listeners of all ages who loved fine gospel singing.

The first challenge

The impact on young people led to the next stage of development in Billy's ministry. In the spring of 1944, Torrey Johnson again approached Billy with an offer. He had booked the 3,000-seat Orchestra Hall in Chicago to hold a 'Youth for Christ' rally.

Above: *Sample page of the kind of hymn George Beverly Shea sang so memorably*

Right: *Billy Graham delivers a radio broadcast in the 1950s*

WMBI—'the oldest Christian radio station in America'

It all started with an accident. In October 1925, guests due to perform for a broadcast on Chicago-based radio station WGES were unable to appear due to a violent storm. Two cornet players, both Moody Bible Institute students, happened to be present in the station and were hastily pressed into service as a last-minute substitution. This set in motion a series of circumstances that led Moody Bible Institute one year later to create its own radio station, WMBI, now the oldest and most well known Christian radio station in America.

In this, the leaders of Moody Bible Institute were following in the innovative steps of its founder, the celebrated evangelist D.L. Moody. When MBI was founded in 1886, Moody had challenged conventional practice with his insistence on the admission of women. He had then charted a new course, even as the founding of WMBI was charting new territory in service to the proclamation of the gospel. It was a visionary venture.

WMBI became the flagship station for a radio network that now consists of some thirty-five commercial free stations. Currently, the Moody Broadcasting Network provides programming via satellite to more than 700 outlets throughout the United States. Early listeners to WMBI could often hear Dr. Harry A. Ironside, the popular pastor of Chicago's Moody Memorial Church. Today, the station presents a full roster of diverse programming: music, talk and call-in shows, news reporting, guided studies of the Scriptures, as well as sermons from noted pastors. But the mission remains the same: to commend the faith. With the advent of satellite technology, the potential listening audience for the Moody Broadcasting Network has increased to well over 30 million people. That violent storm of 1925 proved to be a source of far reaching blessing to untold millions.

This event would specifically target the hundreds of servicemen 'who swept into Chicago every weekend'—men described as 'tough, cynical, sex-starved and indifferent to God and man.' Johnson believed servicemen and unchurched civilians could be reached for Christ 'if clean excitement were linked with an uncompromising Christian message.' Would Billy agree to be the opening night speaker?

Billy Graham immediately consented, but it was a daunting prospect. Yes, a great opportunity had presented itself—but a hall of 3,000? What if he failed as a speaker? What if no one came? These concerns led everyone involved to the place of prayer, and a time of great blessing took place. An estimated 2,800 people were present, most of whom were indeed service personnel. When Billy closed the evening with an invitation to make a commitment for Christ, forty-two people responded. The night had exceeded all expectations, and it created a palpable sense of momentum. By the time of the twenty-first rally, a 20,000-seat stadium had been secured and a new series in Chicago's largest church was planned. Billy now began to travel beyond Chicago, to other large cities like Detroit. His ministry was on the brink of becoming national in scope.

Then came an unforeseen turn of events. In the midst of these developments, Billy had pursued becoming an army chaplain in double harness with his evangelistic ministry. In October 1944 he was commissioned a second lieutenant in the army, and was to begin a chaplains' training course at Harvard Divinity School in Boston. But it was not to be. Billy contracted a virulent case of mumps. His temperature rose

Above: Sailor William Young, the author's grandfather. A symbol of the servicemen for whom Billy Graham and the Youth for Christ team cared so deeply

Left: The Village Church, Western Springs, Illinois, the setting for Billy Graham's first and only pastorate, which lasted from 1943–45

dangerously high, and he became delirious; one night Ruth feared he was dying. Slowly, he recovered, but he was bedridden for six weeks. He grew worryingly thin, and at the end of this time Billy was deeply grateful to receive one hundred dollars to underwrite a trip for further rest in Florida.

As it happened, Torrey Johnson was also in Florida when Billy arrived there. The two friends fished together and talked about the future. Johnson shared his vision for a Youth for Christ movement that could spark a spiritual renewal throughout America, Canada and the world. Could Billy possibly have a place in such a work? His convalescent status meant that he would be assigned to a desk job in the army, a bitter blow, but perhaps it was God's way of closing one door and opening another. After much prayerful consideration, Billy took the painful step of resigning his military commission. It was yet another step of faith, and one he sincerely hoped God would bless.

Youth for Christ

So it proved. In the years immediately following World War II, Youth for Christ experienced a meteoric rise. Rallies were held across the United States, to ever-increasing crowds. Thousands committed their lives to Christ and a whirlwind tour of Europe was undertaken with a view to launching Youth for Christ there. Torrey Johnson marshaled his gift for organization and Billy and other ministry team members joined wholeheartedly in each successive venture of 'daring faith'. But not without controversy. Many clergy in the U.S. feared Youth for Christ might 'divert youth from regular church life'. They were wary of the movement's vitality and methods, and did not understand why Billy, his fellow preachers, and other team members wore loud, hand-painted ties and brightly-colored suits, or why attention-grabbing events were staged, such as an evening when one hundred pianos simultaneously performed a sonata!

In all this, Youth for Christ was taking a page from the methods pioneered by another Chicago-based ministry of an earlier era. D.L. Moody had attracted the children of German and Scandinavian immigrants to his mission with candy and pony rides. To win their parents to Christ, he had organized classes where English was taught. Moody was convinced that 'if you can

Above: *Billy Graham, dynamic preacher for Youth for Christ in the mid 1940s*
Opposite right: *A ticket stub from a Youth for Christ rally*
Opposite left: *Billy Graham, young and stylishly dressed, striking a 'Billy-Sunday-like' pose*

really make a man believe you love him, you have won him.' This could have served as a motto for Billy and his Youth for Christ colleagues. Yet with all this innovative approach, the timeless truths of the gospel were ardently proclaimed, and its ability to transform lives was heralded. Young people responded in ever-increasing numbers. Drawn by the good things that God was doing, there was a passing of the generational baton when Billy Sunday's former song leader, Homer Rodeheaver, preached a guest sermon.

However, the preaching tours could be punishing at times. In 1945 and 1946, having now stepped away from pastoral ministry at the Village Church,

Billy traveled to nearly every state of the Union and every province of Canada. Ruth was expecting their first child, and both came to understand what sacrifice meant in service to the gospel. They missed each other terribly, though it was a comfort for all concerned when Ruth and their little girl, Virginia (nicknamed 'Gigi'), born on 21 September 1945, went to live with Ruth's parents in Montreat, North Carolina.

The Youth for Christ team learned as they journeyed, developing a sensitivity to individual ministry opportunities. It was not always necessary to arrange for elaborate or creative pre-sermon events. Often, when Billy was scheduled to speak, such things were scaled back. The declaration of the gospel was all-important.

Teachable hearts were needed, for zeal sometimes got the better of the team. Once, during a flight layover at an American Air Force base in Newfoundland, the social director for the base asked Torrey Johnson if he and the team could 'give a late night show.' She thought Johnson was the leader of a vaudeville troupe, and Johnson did not disillusion her, given the opportunity for preaching that had just presented itself! In the event, it proved disastrous. The service personnel, thinking they were about to see a cabaret show, were treated instead an evening of gospel singing and speaking. Billy and the team quickly realized their mistake. He apologized for flying under false colors, and shared his testimony. But this did nothing to placate the Base Commander, who was greatly angered. The threat of detainment and a formal enquiry was only forestalled when Wesley Hartzell, a prominent journalist employed by the newspaper magnate William Randolph Hearst, intervened. Hartzell had been traveling with the ministry team, since Hearst had developed a keen interest in the Youth for Christ phenomenon. After everything had been settled, Billy and his friend Chuck Templeton went for a much-needed walk, talking about 'what fools we sometimes were in our zeal.'

The Newfoundland incident well behind them, the team traveled to England, where Billy often took time away from his preaching engagements to reflect. He grew to love the land of his ancestors; England stirred many things within him. Years later he looked back on this time, saying, 'Learning was an insatiable desire with me. I burned to learn, and I felt my limitations of schooling and background so terribly that I determined to try to do all I could through conversations, picking everything I could from everybody.'

Billy had arrived in England with a young man's quick tendency

Above: Ruth Graham and firstborn daughter 'Gigi'

> ### William Randolph Hearst—America's publishing tycoon
>
> Few would have thought that William Randolph Hearst would ever be connected with the start of Billy Graham's national ministry. The two men could not have been more unlike each other. Hearst was a child of privilege. His father had earned a vast fortune from mining interests, and young William was sent to the prestigious St. Paul's Preparatory School and later to Harvard University. Beginning in 1887, while still at Harvard, Hearst was allowed by his father to run the *San Francisco Examiner*. He soon acquired a series of other prominent newspapers. While still a relatively young man, he had amassed an incredibly profitable and influential media empire. At one time, nearly one in four Americans received their news from a Hearst newspaper. Hearst's home city was Los Angeles, where a Youth for Christ chapter had flourished in the post-war years. He became interested in the movement, especially as it provided moral standards for young people and was also a constructive counter to the growing problem of juvenile delinquency. By the time Billy Graham and the Youth for Christ team left for their European tour in March 1946, Hearst had personally approved that articles covering the tour would be distributed through his International News Service, which reached a nationwide audience in America. Hearst was later to play an even more significant role in Billy Graham's rise to national prominence.

to dismiss many of the clergy there as out of touch and tepid in their commitment to the gospel. However, during his stay he came to believe that the genuine revival he longed for there could only come through the mainstream denominations. It was a crucial conclusion, and one which would shape the course of his future ministry in profound ways.

The Canvas Cathedral

By the time the Greater Los Angeles Crusade of September 1949 was launched, Billy Graham's life and ministry had changed in many ways. His family had grown as he, Ruth and eldest daughter Gigi welcomed new baby Anne into the world in May 1948. In that same year, at the age of 29, Billy had been appointed president of Northwestern College in Roseville, Minnesota, where he would serve for four years, until 1952. He was at that time the youngest sitting college president in America.

Left: A front-page story, from 1949, about Billy Graham in the Los Angeles Examiner—*the nationally-influential newspaper founded by media baron William Randolph Hearst*

Above: A front-entrance view of Canvas Cathedral used for the Los Angeles Crusade

The year 1948 could best be described as the year of change. It was then that Billy resigned from the staff of Youth for Christ, though he remained a firm friend of the organization and served for a time on its Board of Trustees. The

Above: A 1940s-era picture of Northwestern Schools in Minneapolis, now Northwestern College—the school for which Billy Graham was appointed President at age 29

reason was this: as opportunities allowed, Billy had begun to hold evangelistic crusades independently of Youth for Christ. This sphere of ministry had grown to such an extent that he decided to devote the whole of his energies to it. As the time of transition unfolded, a new ministry team began to take shape. Billy had already met and worked for a time on the radio program with soloist George Beverly Shea. That collaboration was now renewed, and they were joined by Cliff Barrows, who would serve as a crusade choir director and master of ceremonies; Grady Wilson, whom Billy had known since his childhood days in North Carolina, joined them as associate evangelist.

The Los Angeles Crusade was scheduled to run for three weeks, beginning in late September 1949. Billy sensed early on that this crusade might prove 'a date with destiny', but he had to devote considerable time to convincing the organizing committee of Christ for Greater Los Angeles that it might be so. Their perception was that Billy was simply to serve as their annual evangelist, as others had done in the past. However, Billy had something very different in mind. He wished to secure the use of the largest tent available, work with as many area churches, of whatever denomination, as possible, and triple the allocated budget for the event to an unprecedented

Above: A wide-angle view of the Canvas Cathedral used for the Los Angeles Crusade

$25,000. These might have seemed a set of outlandish requests, but what was at work was a genuine sense of holy boldness informed by an ardent desire to see God change lives on as great a scale as possible—even if that meant defying convention. 'I want to see God sweep in' Billy said, 'because if Los Angeles could have a great revival, the ramifications and repercussions could sweep across the entire world.' For a while the prospects for a Los Angeles crusade 'hung by a thread.' But in the end the planning committee consented to Billy's requests. Everyone concerned bathed the project in prayer, and went to work.

God's blessing soon became evident. The Los Angeles Crusade exceeded expectations, largely due to a series of circumstances no one could have foreseen. A quick summary of what unfolded would be that the crusade 'drew 350,000 people over eight weeks to a huge tent at Washington Boulevard and Hill Street. About 3,000 nonbelievers committed their lives to Christ.' But this is a mere recital of statistics—important though they may be. The story that gave rise to them was fascinating. That the crusade ran for eight weeks and not the original three stemmed in no small measure from an unexpected providence. The newspaper magnate William Randolph Hearst, who had heard many high profile conversions were taking place during the crusades, among them several Hollywood celebrities, sent out a two-word directive to his editors across America: 'Puff Graham'—

Right: Billy and Ruth Graham with Cliff and Billie Barrows during their first trip to England in 1946

that meant, print articles lavishing praise on the crusade. Overnight, it seemed the entire country began talking about the 30-year old preacher and the most celebrated crusade since the heyday of Billy Sunday.

Many years later Billy learned the story behind this extraordinary development from two of Hearst's sons. They always believed 'their father came to the 1949 revival in his wheelchair and in disguise, accompanied by his long time mistress, actress Marion Davies.' In this he seems to have been like many a person who came

Top left: A flyer showing the crowds that flocked to the 1949 Los Angeles Crusade

Below left: An example of how scores of nationally influential newspapers began to 'puff Graham'

What is a 'revival'?

In the United States, the word 'revival' is often synonymous with the words 'mission' or 'crusade'—an evangelistic outreach where the gospel is proclaimed, people are called to repent of their sins, and place their faith in Christ. In the United Kingdom, the word revival is only used to refer to historic outpourings of the Holy Spirit, such as was experienced in the eighteenth century on both sides of the Atlantic under the ministry of Jonathan Edwards, John Wesley, George Whitefield and many others, and again in 1858/59. Billy Graham's use of the word revival is in keeping with traditional usage in America.

Historically, the word 'revival' has several shades of meaning, but it generally refers to a sovereign work of God leading to the renewal or increase of spiritual interest in one church, or in many churches across many geographical boundaries. Historic 'revivals' are viewed against the background of a downgrade of the moral climate of a city, region or country. The hallmarks of spiritual revival are: a widespread conviction of sin leading to repentance and faith in Christ, transformed lives and an upsurge in evangelism and mission. True revival always has a powerful influence upon the morality of the culture at large.

to the crusade: curious and perhaps wondering if what they heard might answer some of life's deepest questions. Whatever drew him, the effect of Hearst's commendation in his newspapers was undeniable: the crusade ran for another five weeks—nearly three times as long as planned. Billy's recollection of the event many years later was one of enduring gratitude: 'I never met [Hearst] and I never corresponded with him. I should have written him and thanked him.'

Lives were transformed as a result of the crusade. Many who had known brokenness and pain found faith, healing and a new life. One of the more moving accounts concerned the former American Olympic track star Lou Zamperini. Zamperini's story reads like a novel. A troubled youth who had several brushes with the law, sport drew him out of a life that threatened to spiral out of control. His Olympic career was no less eventful. He roomed with Jesse Owens at the 1936 Berlin Olympics, stole a Nazi flag from the German chancellery during the Games and shook the hand of Adolf Hitler. During World War II, he survived for forty-seven days on a raft in the Pacific, only to be rescued by the Japanese, who subjected him to horrific treatment as a prisoner of war. 'I fell apart after the war' he recalled. 'I was a drunk. I suffered terrible nightmares and was having marital problems. But my wife was a determined woman who dragged me down to see Graham. I walked out mad the first time. I didn't want to hear that I had sinned. Just to shut her up, I went back.' However, there was something about what he had heard that Zamperini could not shake off. 'I had a flashback about sitting there on the life raft. I had come home alive and never thanked God. I felt terribly ashamed.' He knelt in prayer and surrendered his life to Christ. 'When I got off my knees,' Zamperini said, 'I knew I was through getting drunk. Billy Graham helped save me.'

Hollywood celebrities were curious about the Los Angeles Crusade, among them Spencer Tracy, seated left, and Jimmy Stewart, standing to the right

TRAVEL INFORMATION

Above: Exterior view of the Chicago Avenue Church established by D.L. Moody, circa 1900

Institute

820 N. LaSalle Blvd
Chicago, Illinois 60610
www.moody.edu

The Moody Bible Institute (MBI) is a living legacy to the multifaceted ministry God gave D.L. Moody. Ever faithful to its founder's great commitment to education, MBI welcomes young men and women from all over the world to a setting where they can grow in their faith, even as they are prepared and trained to serve in a wide range of ministry settings. MBI offers an array of undergraduate and graduate degree programs to prepare young men and women for ministry.

MBI is strategically placed for international ministry, inasmuch as several national consulates are located in or close to the Near North Side. The main building of the Consulate-General of the People's Republic of China is in the Near North Side; other countries with consulates similarly situated include Austria, Bosnia and Herzegovina, Brazil, Bulgaria, Chile, Colombia, Denmark, Egypt, Germany, Greece, India, Republic of Ireland, Italy, Japan, South Korea, Lithuania, Poland, Serbia, Switzerland, Thailand, the United Kingdom, and Ukraine.

The River North neighborhood is home of The River North Gallery District, the largest concentration of art galleries in the United States outside of Manhattan. Another region of the River North neighborhood is 'the Cathedral District,' home to Holy Name Cathedral (Catholic) and St. James Cathedral (Episcopal).

MBI is also close to another Chicago neighborhood that many sightseers visit: the Old Town or Old Town Triangle, an historic neighborhood and the site of many Victorian-era buildings. It is also home to St. Michael's Church, originally a Bavarian-built church, and one of 7 to survive the path of the Great Chicago Fire of 1871, which raged from Sunday October 8 to early Tuesday October 10. This devastating event resulted in the death of hundreds of people and destroyed about four square miles of Chicago.

Given its location, is comes as no surprise that a centerpiece of MBI's work is a focus on urban ministry. At the same time, MBI is known internationally as a center for broadcasting (under the aegis of its "flagship" station WMBI) and publishing, through the work of Moody Press. Moody Press has two publishing imprints: Northfield Publishing and Lift Every Voice Books.

The Moody Church

1635 North LaSalle in Chicago, Illinois
www.moodychurch.org
The Moody Church was founded by D.L. Moody and continues to have a vibrant, evangelical ministry in the great urban hub of Chicago. The church website describes its vision for ministry: 'Our vision for The Moody Church is to be known in Chicago as a caring, culturally diverse community that seeks to transform lives through a clear witness for Christ, quality programming, and the lifestyle of each believer.'

The building, completed in 1925, is the largest non-pillared auditorium in the Chicago area and can seat 3,740. It is a fusion of Romanesque and Byzantine architecture and is one of the largest Romanesque churches in America. It is said to possess nearly perfect acoustics. The balcony is one of the earliest examples of cantilevered construction and curves in such a way as to focus all eyes upon the pulpit. Originally, an innovative cooling system was a large pit located in an alley to the rear of the church into which large chunks of ice could be placed; air blown over the ice then flowed through large mushroom-shaped vents under the sanctuary seats. Reportedly, this ingenious system could re-circulate the air throughout the church in six minutes. The chandeliers and thirty-six large stained glass windows are also unique. The auditorium still uses the Reuter organ with some 4,400 pipes in 54 ranks.

Top: A circa 1900 view of the Men's Department Building at the Moody Bible Institute

Below: A circa 1900 view of the Ladies' Department Building at the Moody Bible Institute, originally called the Bible Institute Colportage Association

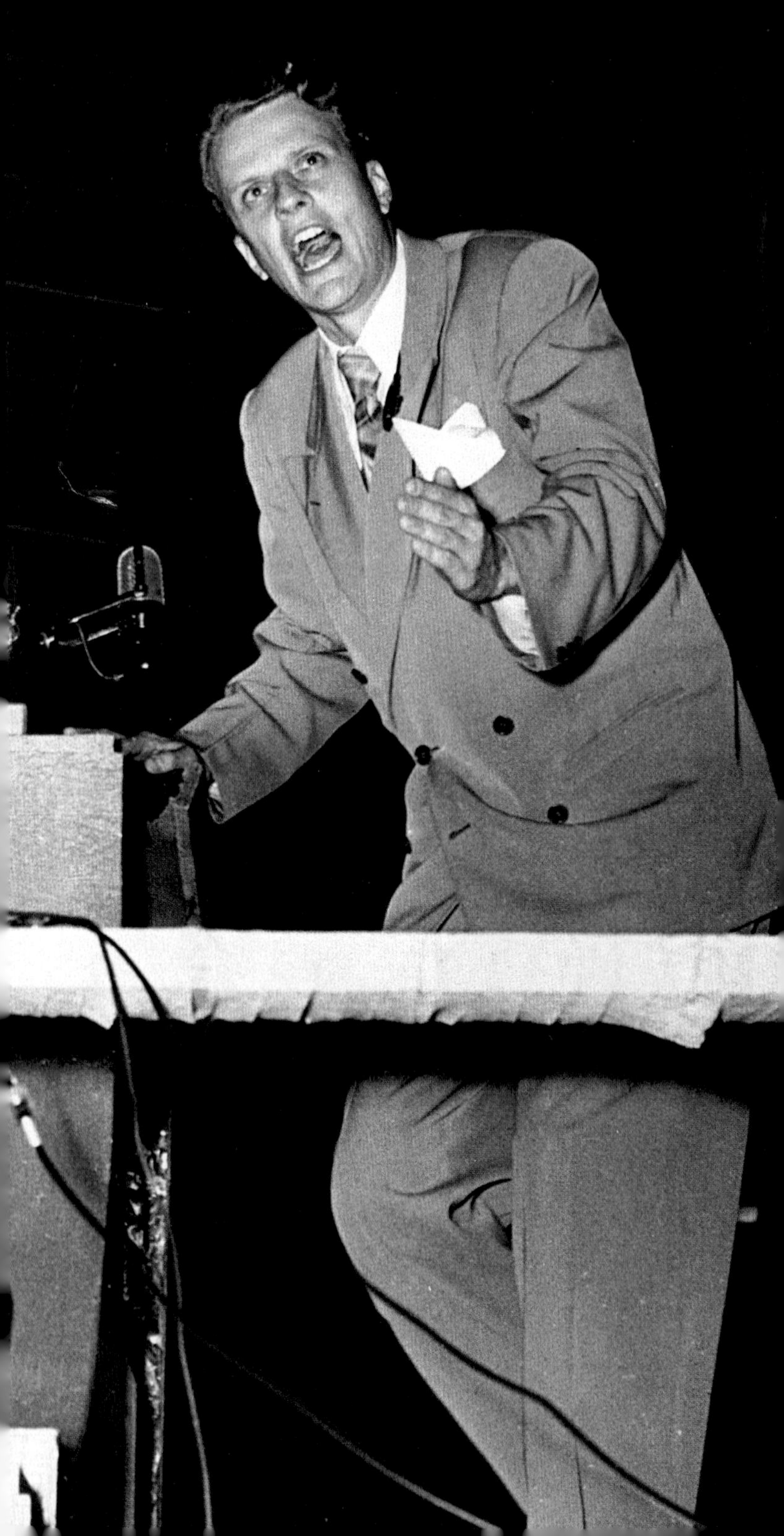

3 A story to tell to the nations

'I am not a great preacher, and I don't claim to be a great preacher. I've heard great preaching many times and wished I was one of those great preachers. I'm an ordinary preacher, just communicating the Gospel in the best way I know how'

As the decade of the 1950s unfolded, Billy Graham's ministry became international. A time of controversy and challenge, it witnessed a celebrated crusade in his ancestral home of Britain, while another in New York City held important implications for race relations.

If the Los Angeles Crusade of 1949 was a high point of Billy Graham's ministry in the 1940s, one of the first significant events of the 1950s proved to be something less. On 14 July 1950 Graham had been invited to the White House by President Truman. Also invited were Cliff Barrows, Jerry Beavan and Grady Wilson. Knowing that Truman was fond of stylish summer suits; each man wore similar attire to the meeting, along with white buckskin shoes. Though well intended, it was a rather showy display. However, their meeting with the President was cordial, lasting twenty minutes. At its end, Graham asked to lead everyone in a moment of prayer. The president replied, 'Well, I don't suppose any harm could be done by that.' As Graham prayed, his words were seconded by an occasional 'Amen' from Barrows—which became 'Do it Lord!' when petitions were offered for the President himself. As soon as they left the President, the press surrounded Graham and his friends, shoving and yelling in their eagerness to learn what had taken place. What followed has been described by Graham biographer John Pollock as an 'eruption of boyish immaturity', Billy told the reporters 'everything I could remember' about his conversation with the President. He then agreed

Above: *Billy Graham, studying his Bible*

Facing Page: *Billy Graham's energetic preaching often left him exhausted and he learned to trust in God for his strength*

Above: Billy Graham's self-described 'embarrassing experience' following his meeting with President Truman on 14 July 1950

to kneel with his friends on the White House lawn as though re-enacting the time of prayer with Truman. Photographers eagerly snapped pictures. When President Truman learned of this, he was understandably deeply angry. He called the young preacher a 'counterfeit' and a publicity-seeker. It was a hard lesson that Graham never forgot. 'Now I was persona non grata at the White House,' he recalled. 'Mr. Truman never asked me to come back.'

Several months later, in December 1950, a far happier event took place. The Graham family welcomed a third daughter, Ruth, into the fold. Meanwhile, another ministry milestone occurred. In September of the same year, The Billy Graham Evangelistic Association (BGEA) was incorporated—a tax-exempt organization whereby funds could be raised to support the work of ministry. In November, the BGEA took an initial step in what became a continuing, innovative stewardship of media technology—radio broadcasts of the *Hour of Decision* program began.

Inspiration from Moody

A visit in April 1950 to D.L. Moody's grave in Northfield, Massachusetts, reflected Graham's desire to pay tribute to a man whose life and ministry he deeply admired. This graveside visit also foreshadowed a controversy with which Graham would soon be confronted. The context was this: during a ministry that reached millions for Christ, Moody had gratefully worked alongside Christians of different

Above: The White House, home of America's presidents, and a place Billy Graham has visited many times

The White House

Home to every chief executive since America's second president, John Adams, (inset) the White House was constructed in the late Georgian style between 1792 and 1800. During the presidency of Thomas Jefferson, the White House was remodeled to include two colonnades extending outward using a design supplied by the British-born American architect Benjamin Henry Latrobe, also famous for his design for the U.S. Capitol and the renovations to Barham Court in Kent, England. So celebrated was Latrobe in his adopted homeland that he came to be regarded as 'the father of American architecture'.

Important modifications to the White House have taken place down through the years. In 1901, President Theodore Roosevelt oversaw the construction of the West Wing, while his successor William Howard Taft supervised the construction of the first Oval Office. Other renovations have included the construction of the East Wing, primarily the site used as a reception area on social occasions. Early names for the White House, included the 'President's Palace', and the 'Presidential Mansion'. It was not until 1901 that President Roosevelt had the words 'White House—Washington' engraved on his official stationery. The White House is owned by the National Park Service, which regularly conducts tours of the parts of the residence that are open to the public.

Inset: John Adams, circa 1800, the first president to reside in The White House

Above: The 'memorial plaque' for D.L. Moody that serves as the frontispiece for W.R. Moody's 1900 biography. 'Some day you will read that D.L. Moody is dead. Don't you believe a word of it! At that moment I shall be more alive than I am now…'

denominational backgrounds. He would also preach anywhere—be it a hippodrome in New York, a music hall or theatre—provided he could proclaim the gospel freely. God's blessing upon Moody's ministry was powerfully evident in 1873, during crusades held in Edinburgh, Scotland. As Professor W.G. Blaikie recalled at the time: 'It would be difficult to enumerate the ministers who have taken a prominent and most hearty interest in the movement. The utter absence of jealousy, the cordial cooperation of the clergy of all denominations in the work, has been extremely striking.'

Moody's son William described one unforgettable night: 'On

Below: D.L. Moody, *a herald of grace and mercy for crowds of unprecedented size—and the spiritual role model for Billy Graham*

Also: D.L. Moody *preaching at Haymarket during one of his tours of Britain*

Sunday evening the Free Assembly Hall, the Established Assembly Hall, and the Free High Church were all filled to overflowing, as well as Free St. John's Church. All denominational differences were forgotten. Professor Charteris spoke in the Free Church; Professor Blaikie spoke in the Established Church. Brethren from all parts of the country came together in the unity of a common need and a common Saviour.' As a result, a circular letter was sent to every minister in Scotland, which stated: 'Edinburgh is now enjoying signal manifestations of grace…the Free Church Assembly Hall, the largest public building in Edinburgh, is crowded every evening with meetings for prayer, and both that building and the Established Church Assembly Hall overflow whenever the Gospel is preached. But the numbers that attend are not the most remarkable feature. It is the presence and power of the Holy Ghost…'

This was to be Billy's model. His willingness to reach across party lines, whether religious or political, had earlier borne good fruit and would continue. For example, in 1952, the BGEA had received an invitation from Democratic and Republican senators and representatives to hold a five-week crusade in Washington, D.C. Present at this crusade was Colin Kerr, a Prebendary of St. Paul's Cathedral, London. Kerr's Anglican faith tradition was poles apart from Graham's Baptist faith tradition, but he was deeply impressed by the respect accorded Graham from national leaders, and the people from all walks of life who made their way to the counseling room to give their lives to Christ. 'It was a work of God's Spirit,' Kerr recalled, 'and not just an overawing by a great and fascinating personality.' The crusade culminated in a moving service held on Sunday, February 3 on the steps of the Capitol building in Washington—following the passage of an unprecedented Act of Congress allowing it to take

Above: *Billy Graham with sons Franklin (right) and Ned in the early 1960s*

place. Across America, radio and television stations carried the service live. Graham read President Lincoln's 1863 proclamation for a day of humiliation and prayer. With war then raging in Korea, he stated in his message that a new day of humiliation and prayer should be proclaimed. It was vital, he said, that the nation 'return to God, the Bible [and] the Church.'

In July 1952, Ruth and Billy Graham welcomed their fourth child and first son Franklin into their family (their fifth and last child, Ned, would arrive six years later). The following year, 1953, would prove no less eventful than 1952. It was then that Graham began publicly and repeatedly to declare his opposition to racial segregation. This principled stand cost him friends and brought scorn upon him from people still held in prejudice. 'Jesus Christ belongs to all races', Graham declared, 'there are no color lines with Christ… God looks upon the heart.'

Harringay, London 1954

Another place and another people close to Graham's heart were the people of Britain. His visit there immediately after World War II had stirred him deeply. Now, as the mid 1950s approached, God opened the door for the BGEA to schedule an extended evangelistic

Below: *Billy Graham and Civil Rights pioneer Dr. Martin Luther King, Jr.*

Above: Billy Graham's welcome at Waterloo Station in London, January 1954

outreach there. So, one year after the coronation of Queen Elizabeth II, from March 1 through to May 22 1954 the Greater London or Harringay Crusade took place. If there was a watchword for this time of ministry, it was well expressed in Graham's declaration: 'This is the hour of the church in England.'

However, at the outset, the prospects for a mighty moving of the Spirit of God among the people of Britain seemed remote. Skepticism was the order of the day for many—notably, members of the press. One prominent newspaper, *The People,* spoke for all of the publications that sought to 'debunk Graham' when it declared: 'Must we be turned into better citizens and kinder husbands by the antics of Billy Graham's American hot gospel circus?… Being bulldozed into loving God by ecstatic young men who talk about him with easy familiarity is something which makes the biggest British sinner shudder. When the cheer leader of the troupe turns out to be as ignorant of British history as Billy Graham, we are entitled to protest. He would have done more good for his cause by staying away and sending over the money that would have been saved on the fares to buy candy for our poor kids.'

The prospects were no better when the day of the first meeting at Harringay arrived. While Billy and the BGEA team readied themselves for the event in prayer and consultation at their small hotel near Oxford Circus, discouraging news was conveyed to them. Just one hour before the meeting was to begin, Ruth Graham sat writing in her diary when a sober faced Billy came in. He had just received word that 'there aren't more than 2,000 people at Harringay [an arena which seated 11,400] and around 200 or 300 hundred newspaper men, television cameras, newsreels and so on.' As Ruth recalled: 'Billy looked sort of stunned when he told me.' He then retired to pray in an adjoining room. Upon arrival at the Harringay arena a short time later, things looked no better.

The forecourt was empty. All Billy and Ruth could see were 'crowds streaming towards the greyhound stadium beyond.' He turned to her and said: 'Let's go face it and believe that God has a purpose in it.'

What unfolded in the next few moments came as a shock. They were met at their car by their friend Willis Haymaker, who told them hurriedly: 'The Arena is jammed! It is full and running over, and thousands are on the other side!' As Billy and Ruth entered the arena, they were met with the glad sound of hymns reverberating throughout, and two American Senators, smiling broadly. They had excused themselves early from a meeting with Prime Minister Winston Churchill, and were due to leave shortly for a formal dinner hosted by the American Ambassador. Be that as it may, they declared they had come 'determined to speak on [your] behalf.'

That night 178 people, mostly young persons, gave their life to Christ when Graham made his invitation to come forward. It was a glorious harbinger of what was to come. Britons in their thousands came and came, extra meetings had to be scheduled frequently and 'full up' signs were the rule for the entire three months of the crusade. As John Pollock has observed, the mission to London 'was bringing forward enquirers in numbers that America had produced only at the climax of a crusade.' Something truly extraordinary was unfolding, and years later Graham himself recalled: 'If our 1949 meetings in Los Angeles marked a decisive watershed for our ministry in the United States, the London Crusade in 1954 did the same for us internationally. News of what had happened at Harringay travelled like lightning around the world, challenging Christians to believe that the particular place where God had put them was not beyond hope,

Right: *A sample of the highly skeptical press Billy Graham initially received upon his arrival in England*

but that He was still at work.'

A bare recital of statistics would tell that attendance numbers for the Harringay Crusade exceeded two million people. On the final day of the crusade, Billy preached to an estimated two hundred thousand people—the largest religious gathering in British history. Some 38,000 people were said to have come forward to make a profession of faith in Christ as Savior. Demand for seating for the final meeting of the crusade was such that use of the renowned outdoor stadium at Wembley, had to be secured. The Lord Mayor of London would be present for this occasion, and the Archbishop of Canterbury, Geoffrey Fisher, would give the invocation. All this conveys some sense of the phenomenon that the crusade had become, but the most telling and by far the most important fact to emerge from this unfolding of God's work in Britain was the lives of so many Britons that were changed. So many had experienced either a renewal of their faith, or placed their faith in Christ. As Graham recalled: 'thousands of lives had been touched with the transforming message of Jesus Christ. We [also] knew that even among those who made no decision during the meetings, seeds had been planted that would bear fruit in God's timing.' Even the vendors on the London tube caught the significance of the event by selling 'Billy Graham peanuts' with the slogan 'Come and be saved, you look like you need it'!

Another source of blessing for Graham and the BGEA team was the knowledge that churches throughout Britain had been strengthened. The Archbishop of Canterbury concurred in this view: 'That the blessing of the Holy Spirit had been upon this campaign cannot be doubted…The mission has beyond doubt brought new strength and hope in Christ to multitudes, and won many to him; and for this, God is to be praised. It has given an impetus to evangelism for which all the Churches may be thankful to God.'

The capstone to the Harringay crusade took place in two parts,

Above left: *Billy Graham, preaching before a huge crowd at Trafalgar Square on 3 April 1954. It was the largest crowd in the Square since the celebrations of VE day in May 1945*

Left: *Billy Graham with Geoffrey Fisher, Archbishop of Canterbury*

Above: Interior view of the Harringay Crusade at its height

an invitation to preach before Queen Elizabeth II on May 22, and a chance to meet with Prime Minister Churchill on May 24. To preach before the Queen was a very high privilege, but it was the impromptu invitation to meet with the Prime Minister that produced the most unexpected and memorable results. It seemed that curiosity had gotten the better of the PM. He had received regular updates of what was unfolding during the Harringay Crusade via press clippings and briefing from media relations members of his staff. Consequently, an invitation to Graham was extended for a five minute meeting. Civilities could be exchanged, and the Prime Minister could see for himself what Graham was like. Graham arrived at Number 10, Downing Street, at noon on Monday May 24. He had no way of knowing, but Mr. Churchill was somewhat at a loss as to how he should greet his young American guest. 'What do you talk to an American evangelist about?' he wondered aloud. Graham was shown through to the Cabinet Room, whereupon Churchill asked him to be seated. The Prime Minister spoke first, saying he had been following all that was taking place at Harringay. He was glad Graham and his team had come to England, 'because we need this emphasis.' Then, unexpectedly, came a startling question. 'Do you have any hope?' Churchill asked. 'What hope do you have for the world?' Many young men being ushered into the presence of such a great man could be forgiven for being at a loss for words in the face of questions like this. Graham was grateful ever after that God helped him to reply. Quietly, Graham withdrew from his pocket the little New Testament he always carried. Looking down to it he said, 'Mr. Prime Minister, I am filled with hope.'

There followed a remarkable exchange. Churchill pointed to a nearby table where the headlines of early editions of London newspapers were there for him to see. These papers, the Prime Minister said are 'filled with rapes, murders, and hate.' It had not been like this when he was a boy, and now things seemed so changed—so noisy and violent. Then there was the constant concern over the growing Communist menace in so many places. More than once, the Prime Minister commented, 'I am an old man, without hope for the world.' All Graham knew to do was to say that despite such dire tidings; he was nonetheless filled with hope 'because I know what is going to happen in the future.' He then began to speak of Christ, referring at times to relevant passages in his pocket New Testament that spoke of Jesus' birth, death, resurrection and ascension—and what it meant to be born again. He did so, feeling a mixture of inward agitation and amazement that his five-minute meeting had suddenly turned so consequential. As Graham spoke, his best impression was that Churchill seemed quite receptive, speaking seldom, choosing to rather to listen.

Graham continued to speak as though he were counseling a young inquirer about spiritual things at Harringay. 'Christ will return', he declared, 'He will come again.' Five minutes became forty. At the meeting's close, the Prime Minister told his guest, 'I do not see much hope for the future unless it is the hope you are talking about, young man. We must have a return to God.' He then stepped out of his reflective mood to treat Graham to a dose of Churchillian humor. Shaking Graham's hand, he said, 'Our conversation is private, isn't it?' The Prime Minister had been aware of Graham's naïve behavior in betraying conversational details when meeting President Truman some years before, and couldn't resist a bit of good-natured ribbing. Graham's smile at this might have been a bit rueful, but the recollections of Churchill's private secretaries after the PM's death were what mattered most. Their recollection was that Churchill had been 'terribly impressed,' and had found Billy Graham 'most interesting and agreeable.'

One experience from the Harringay Crusade that would later play a prominent role in Billy Graham's ministry was his introduction to a teenager named David Frost. Looking back on this first meeting, Graham recalled: 'One of the ablest interviewers I have known is David Frost. We first met when he came to our 1954 meetings in London's Harringay Arena. David's father was a Methodist preacher, and

Above: Sir Winston Churchill, with whom Billy Graham had an unexpectedly lengthy and cordial meeting on 24 May 1954

Above: Billy Graham, after his 'five-minute' meeting with Prime Minister Winston Churchill in 1954. The details of which he revealed only after Churchill's death

Harringay Arena

When Billy Graham scheduled a series of crusades at Harringay Arena in 1954, many wondered if he and his colleagues had been foolish to do so. Located in what has been described as 'a drab section of North London,' it had previously been a venue for boxing matches, ice hockey games and circuses. It was adjacent to a track for dog racing, and amidst such a setting many asked, 'Would people come?' Any such concerns proved entirely unfounded. Not only was the arena full to bursting on the first night of the crusade, it was to be the scene of capacity or near capacity crowds for weeks in succession. Throughout its multipurpose history, Harringay Arena was also the scene for classical music concerts and ballet performances. The face that this venue presented to the public was unusual. Octagonal in shape, it owed its rather spare modernist design to Dr. Oscar Faber, a British architect and consulting engineer. Cultural critics may have disdained the use of a pedestrian setting for concerts and ballet performances, but there is no doubt that the use of the arena for such events allowed many more people to experience these forms of art than might otherwise have been able to.

Just four years after the Billy Graham crusades were held, the last event was staged at the arena: a lightweight boxing match between Dave Charnley and Carlos Ortiz. Following this, the arena was used as a food storage warehouse until it was demolished in 1978. However inglorious its final days may have been, there is no doubt that the arena earned a significant place in Christian history as the scene of one of the great spiritual renewal movements of the twentieth century.

Left: A montage of issues of Christianity Today, *the magazine founded by Billy Graham and Carl Henry*

New York 1957

As the 1950s drew to a close, the other watershed ministry for the BGEA was the New York Crusade of 1957. It was an event that Billy Graham and his team had long contemplated and for which they cherished high hopes. On the eve of this crusade, Graham met with President Eisenhower in Washington, D.C. What unfolded during that brief meeting is reflective of how deeply the ministry God had given Graham and the BGEA team had touched a chord among many Americans, not least the nation's chief executive. Eisenhower, it seems, had already read about plans for the New York Crusade. He told Graham 'It would be wonderful if people all over the world could love each other.' The President's words provided Graham with a chance to affirm what Christianity teaches in this regard. He told Eisenhower that 'The gospel has a vertical as well as a horizontal aspect, that men must be born again and be truly converted before they have the capacity to love.' It was a source of tremendous encouragement to hear the President respond immediately after this that he heartily agreed. The New York Crusade, which was one of the lengthier crusades in the BGEA's history, lasted from May 15 through to September 1. From the start it received significant media coverage. Walter Cronkite,

his mother spent a vacation with Ruth and me in our home.'

Media ministry of another kind unfolded in the development of the BGEA when Billy Graham, together with the Christian writer and theologian Carl Henry, founded the influential magazine *Christianity Today* in 1956. Over time, this widely respected periodical became the *Time* magazine of evangelicals in America. It chronicled the growth of evangelicalism throughout the US and abroad and increasingly brought an evangelical perspective to bear on news events and cultural trends. Still flourishing, CT, as it is affectionately known, remains a widely influential periodical for those who seek to understand evangelical Christianity or to think Christianly about the world in which we live. Over time, CT has launched sister publications such as *Christian History* and *Books & Culture*. It is also published online via the world wide web.

Above: Billy Graham with President Eisenhower in the 1950s

Above: Billy Graham taping a television interview during the New York Crusade in 1957

then revered as 'America's news anchor', conducted an interview with Graham that aired on the CBS Evening News—the premier news program in the US at this time.

Another milestone was reached when live television broadcasts of Graham's sermons began at this time. They aired throughout the US and marked the effective start of what came to be called the 'televangelism era'. This was unquestionably important, but it paled in significance to the service that was held during the New York City Crusade on 18 July 1957. It was then that Dr. Martin Luther King, Jr. led the assembled congregants in prayer. Such a thing was unheard of at that time, but it marked the start of a cordial friendship between the two Christian leaders and was in itself a major step forward in racial integration. The numbers too were groundbreaking for the New York Crusade. The final total of attendance throughout the various venues—Madison Square Garden, Yankee Stadium and Times Square—was 2,357,400 the highest attendance number recorded up to that time for a BGEA crusade. Best of all, the number of 'decisions' for Christ was 61,148. God had richly blessed all of the prayer, hard work and planning that the BGEA and so many collegial groups had invested in this crusade. A ministry of international scope had emerged and would continue to grow in the decades ahead.

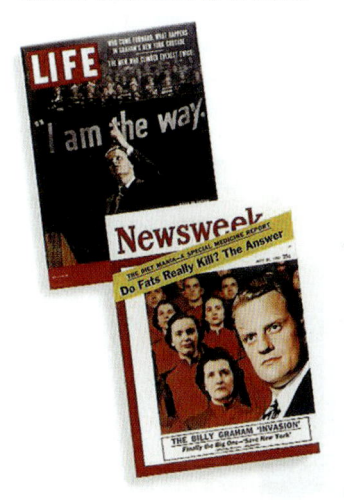

Above: Samples of the press coverage Billy Graham received during the New York Crusade

TRAVEL INFORMATION

Harringay

Located just under 5 miles (8.7 km) from the center of London, Harringay is a residential area of North London, in the London Borough of Haringey. Since 1750, it has been celebrated as a recreational destination for Londoners. Down through the years, Harringay has been home to many popular leisure destinations, among them Hornsey Wood House, Finsbury Park, Harringay Stadium and Harringay Arena. The sites formerly occupied by the Harringay Stadium and Arena are now occupied by Sainsbury's and the Arena Shopping Mall.

Green space land is still a feature that draws visitors to Harringay. Popular sites to visit are Finsbury Park, the Railway Fields Local Nature Reserve (near Harringay Green Lanes Station), and the New River Path, which is accessible from Green Lanes opposite Finsbury Park. Harringay is also home to two church sites representative of the ancient and the modern. Of ancient renown is the Hornsey Church, distinguished by its 13th century church tower. A church built in the modernist style is St Paul's Church and Vicarage located on Wightman Road, described by Simon Jenkins of *The Guardian* as a 'dazzling' place of worship. Many look on St. Paul's as an architectural achievement in its own right, aside from its primary function as a church.

The nearest tube stations are Manor House and Turnpike Lane. For those arriving by bus, there are three major bus routes that connect Green Lanes with the City and the West End: the 29, 141, and the 341. The nearby Turnpike Lane bus station offers further connection to the west, east and north.

The Smithsonian Institution

The Smithsonian Institution (SI), Washington, D.C.
website: www.si.edu/visit
For those visiting Washington DC, the SI is a must. Home to 19 museums and 9 research centers. As such it is a centerpiece of American culture and history. It has an Anglo-American pedigree. It came into being as a result of a bequest made by James Smithson a wealthy British mineralogist and chemist who was also a Fellow of the Royal Society. Smithson's bequest, which serves today as the mission statement for SI, reads: 'I...bequeath the whole of my property... to the United States of America, to found at Washington, under the name of the

Left: *Exterior view of the Harringay Arena at the time of the Billy Graham Crusade in 1954*

Above: *John Quincy Adams, whose patient diplomacy made The Smithsonian Institution a reality*

Smithsonian Institution, an Establishment for the increase and diffusion of knowledge…' The SI's website describes the nature of Smithson's munificent gift: 'In September 1838, Smithson's legacy, which amounted to more than 100,000 gold sovereigns, was delivered to the mint at Philadelphia. Re-coined in U.S. currency, the gift amounted to more than $500,000.'

Within the Smithsonian complex: The **Anacostia Community Museum** celebrates the history and culture of African-American communities. The **Cooper-Hewitt National Design Museum** features a continually changing set of exhibitions of design, decorative arts, industrial design and architecture. The **Freer Gallery of Art** and **Arthur M. Sackler Gallery** is a facility that specializes in Asian and American art. The **Hirshhorn Museum** and **Sculpture Garden** is a center for modern and contemporary art. The **National Air and Space Museum** traces the history, science and technology of aviation and space flight. The **National Museum of American History** is a repository dedicated to the history of science, technology, society and culture in America. The **National Museum of Natural History** encompasses all things relating to the natural history of America. The **National Museum of the American Indian** centers its work on the collection, preservation, study and exhibition of the living cultures and history of the native peoples of the Americas. The **National Portrait Gallery** houses portraits of distinguished Americans. The national **Zoological Park** is home to more than 400 animal species in a 163-acre park. The **Smithsonian American Art Museum** and its **Renwick Gallery** serve as a repository for painting, sculpture, graphics, folk art, craft and photography from the 18th century to the present. Lastly, the **Smithsonian Institution Building**, the Castle, serves as the Smithsonian Information Center.

Right: *The Smithsonian Castle, centerpiece of the Smithsonian Institution*

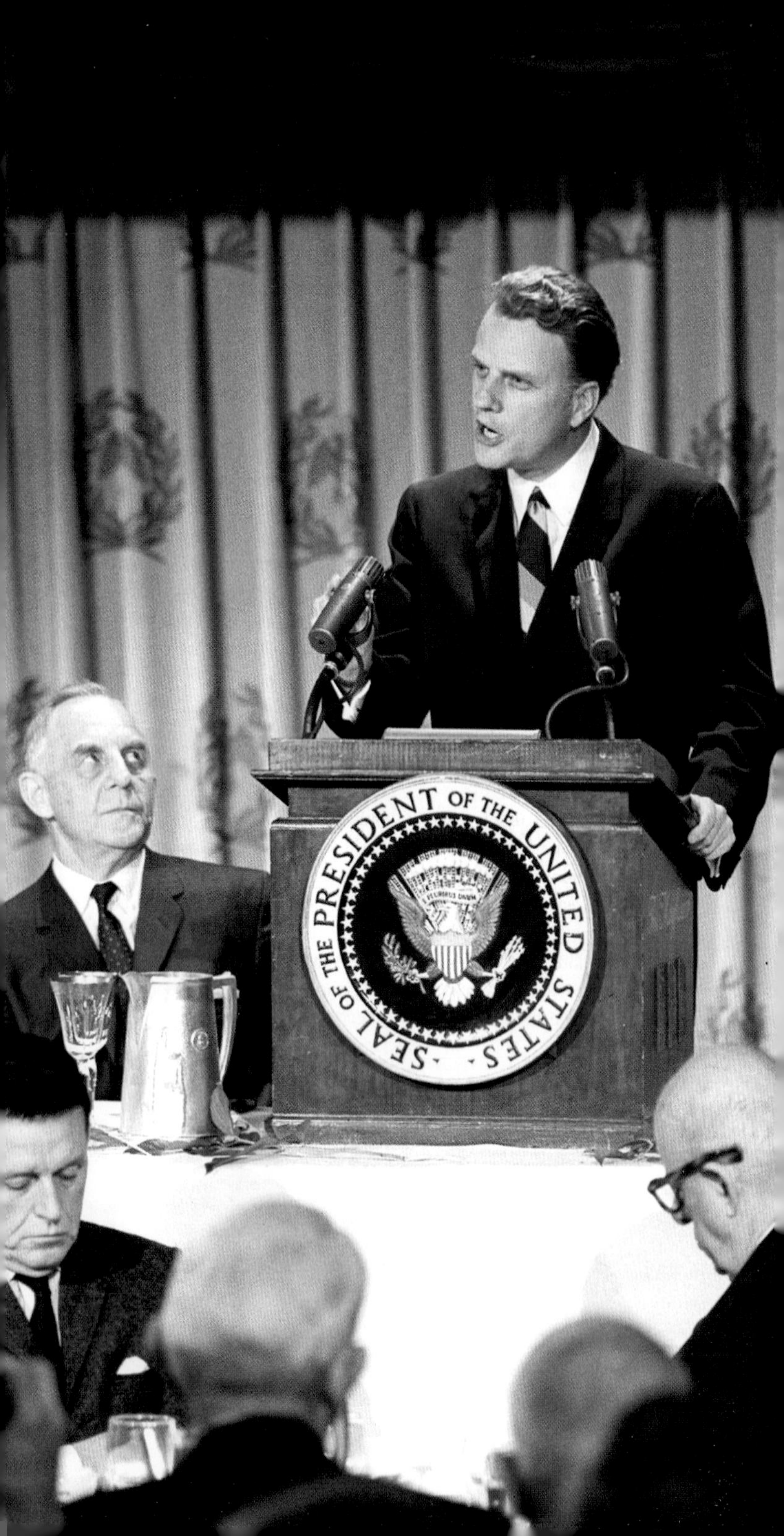
SEAL OF THE PRESIDENT OF THE UNITED STATES

❹ New opportunities—troubled horizons

'When I was young, I sometimes wanted to answer all my critics. Now, I just leave them with the Lord. If I tried to answer every critic that's all I would have time to do. But God has called me to preach and be about the business of winning the lost'

Opposition from all sides

By the early 1950s, the BGEA had for some time been engaged in Moody-style crusade planning. As the ministry's leader, Graham was the focus of censure from liberal and conservative Christians alike. From the liberal side, *The Christian Century* magazine stated: 'The Billy Graham campaign will spin along … an audience gladly captive to its own sensations is straining for the grand entrance…whether or not the Holy Spirit is in attendance.' Theologian Reinhold Niebuhr also criticized Graham, saying he was 'obviously sincere' but that his message was 'too simple in any age, but particularly so in a nuclear one with its great moral perplexities.' For his part, Graham appreciated Niebuhr's commitment to social concern but 'could not agree with his scorn of evangelism.' Seeking to extend a hand of friendship, Graham requested a meeting on two occasions but was rebuffed. Niebuhr refused to see him.

When it came to conservative opposition, biographer John Pollock described Graham's predicament in this way:

'Certain conservatives such as Dr. John R. Rice and Dr. Carl McIntire pronounced him guilty of association with men of false beliefs on the Bible, the Atonement and other "fundamentals of the faith"; he should separate himself from all who were unsound… Billy Graham could not believe it Christ's will that he should

Above: *General (later President) Dwight D. Eisenhower. On the eve of Eisenhower's passing, Billy Graham counselled him to place his faith in Christ*

Facing page: *Billy Graham addressing the National Prayer Breakfast in 1963*

treat every supporter of the National Council of Churches as a theological leper; moreover he knew modernists whose beliefs and ministry had been revolutionised by taking part in an uncompromisingly evangelical crusade. The fundamentalist critics did not seek out Billy Graham "to counsel with me, pray with me, talk with me [or to] love me'; they wrote cold, hard, demanding letters, and articles." He was tempted to reply, but soon adopted, on a hint from V. Raymond Edman [the President of Wheaton College], the policy expressed to critics by Nehemiah: "I am doing a great work, so that I cannot come down: why should the work cease, whilst I leave it, and come down to you?"'

Graham himself, looking back on this time in his ministry, has reflected: 'My study of the major evangelists in history showed me that the issue was not new; every one of them—from Whitefield and Wesley to Moody and Sunday—had to contend with similar criticisms, both from the right and from the left... My own position was that we should be willing to work with all who were willing to work with us. Our message was clear, and if someone with a radically different theological view somehow decided to join with us in a Crusade that proclaimed Christ as the way of salvation, he or she was the one who was compromising personal conviction, not we.'

Above: *Billy Graham and President John F. Kennedy in 1961 at a National Prayer Breakfast*

Right: Billy Graham and President Kennedy (far left) at a National Prayer Breakfast in 1963. One year before the President's assassination

A call from John F Kennedy

In April 1960, Billy Graham received an unexpected phone call. On the line was John F. Kennedy, the Democratic Party presidential candidate. Would he, Senator Kennedy wanted to know, be willing to say that he would not hesitate to vote for a Catholic candidate for president, provided he was qualified? Graham declined to make a public statement as he had resolved not to endorse any specific candidate, but he did say that he saw no serious problem with the idea of a Catholic in the White House. The response of some Protestants was inevitable. Some feared that a president who greatly respected the authority of the pope might be deferential to papal authority in matters of policy; many Baptists, in particular, held a deep distrust for anything they thought verged on a blurring of the line of separation between church and state. With hindsight, such fears proved groundless, but as there had never been a Catholic president in America, such fears occasionally gave way to strident and hurtful anti-catholic pronouncements.

When Senator Kennedy was elected president, Graham got to know him and several members of his family. Privately, he had voiced support for Richard Nixon. But Kennedy had won and now there were new opportunities for ministry created by that turn of events. Over the years of Kennedy's presidency, there were occasionally serious discussions of religious topics. On one memorable occasion, the then president-elect asked Graham several questions about the second coming of Christ. At the close of their talk, Kennedy said 'We'll have to talk more about that someday.' Other opportunities did arise. One concerned the Peace Corps, formed by President Kennedy and led by Sargent Shriver. Over time, Graham became

Above: Late November, 1963, a time when all America mourned; an image from the funeral service for President Kennedy

quite familiar with this service agency's work and took an active role along with Shriver in the production of a documentary exploring the problem of poverty in the Appalachian Mountains. The opportunity to reach out a hand in friendship to a new administration also extended to a National Prayer Breakfast at which Graham spoke and President Kennedy attended. Invitations to the White House were also then extended periodically. When President Kennedy was tragically shot in Dallas, Texas, on 22 November 1963, Graham keenly felt the sense of shock and grief shared by America and the world. What made things worse was that for days prior to the assassination, Graham had felt a deep sense of foreboding about the Dallas trip. He had tried to contact Kennedy directly to tell him this, but was unsuccessful. As he later recalled: 'All I wanted to tell…the President was one thing—don't go to Texas!'

The logo of the Peace Corps, a federal service organization with which Billy Graham became actively involved in its early days

Sir David Frost

Born on 7 April 1939, Sir David Frost is the son a Methodist minister, the Rev. W.J. Paradine Frost. As a young man, Frost himself commenced training as a Methodist Local Preacher, but other pursuits and interests prompted him to cease before it was completed.

A gifted athlete, he was once offered a contract with Nottingham Forest Football Club. Instead, he chose to attend university at Gonville and Caius College, Cambridge, where he had won a place as a result of high academic performance at the Wellingborough Grammar School.

Following his time at university, Frost commenced a career in television, where his gifts as a witty and incisive social satirist, presenter and interviewer soon became evident. During the 1960s, he hosted a widely popular program called *That Was The Week That Was*—commonly known in its time as 'TW3'. Perhaps the most famous episode of this program was the tribute Frost gave to President John F. Kennedy following his assassination in November 1963. This brought Frost notoriety in US, and led eventually to the start of the program Frost on America. In this capacity, Frost interviewed a diverse array of public figures, among them comedian Jack Benny and playwright Tennessee Williams. Most famously, Frost conducted a series of hard-hitting interviews with former President Richard Nixon, which were followed with great attention in the wake of the Watergate scandal.

Over the years, Frost has also conducted many interviews with Billy Graham, beginning in 1964. These are memorable in their own right, and well worth viewing (or reading, as their transcripts are reproduced in Frost's book *Billy Graham in Conversation*, Lion Publishing, 1998). But perhaps the most prominent example of Sir David's appreciation for Graham can be found in the DVD documentary *Billy Graham: God's Ambassador* (20th Century Fox, 2006), which Frost hosted and narrated with great warmth and respect.

Left: Sir David Frost, who once praised Billy Graham for being 'vibrantly alive and flagrantly Christian' and wished he had stayed longer in the U.K to further extend the work of the Harringay Crusade. Here interviewing Billy Graham in Australia in 1979

Left: A powerful, if little known victory for civil rights in the American South: Billy Graham crusades were integrated and reflective of how the love of Christ can bridge racial divides

Racial tension

The collective grief that enveloped America proved a sad prelude to the social upheaval that persisted throughout the remainder of the decade. As these events unfolded, Billy Graham would be at or near the center of many of them. One of the first was the dramatic increase in racial tensions as Freedom Marches began to be held throughout the American south. Graham did not take part in these events, but he consistently called for 'mutual tolerance, conciliation, and the necessity to strike at the root of the matter.' As he explained: 'The race question will not be solved by demonstrations in the streets, but in the hearts of both Negro and White. There must be genuine love to replace prejudice and hate. This love can be supplied by Christ—and only by Christ.'

Then, on 15 September 1963, Birmingham, Alabama's 16th Street Baptist Church was bombed. It was an act of racially motivated terrorism in which four African-American children were killed. People across the nation were horrified and grief stricken. In the wake of this tragedy, Billy Graham offered to bring the BGEA team to Birmingham, bringing the message of Christ's love—a love that can heal the deepest wounds. He had, however, one condition. 'The meeting,' he said, 'must be integrated. We would not come otherwise. If we can't meet at the cross of Christ as brothers, we can't make it in other areas.' It took a while for all the arrangements to be made, but on Easter Sunday 1964, the BGEA held a rally at Birmingham's Legion Field.

Above: An interior view of a session from the Lausanne World Congress on Evangelism, an event for which Billy Graham and other Christian leaders like John Stott were a guiding inspiration over several days, from 16–25 July 1974

35,000 people came. Half of those in attendance were black and half were white—making this event the largest integrated event in the state's history. Much remained to be done to improve race relations in this troubled place, but the BGEA had done what it could to make a start, and had done so by saying 'there's room at the cross for all.'

World Evangelization

Throughout the 1960s, the BGEA continued to build on the international ministry established during the Harringay Crusade just a few years before. Graham and his team scheduled over 100 crusades across the world: in London, Tokyo, the former Yugoslavia, Brazil, and in major cities in Canada and the United States. This international emphasis on the proclamation of the gospel was seen perhaps most strongly in 1966, when the World Congress on Evangelism was held in West Berlin, Germany.

Though inaugurated and funded largely by the BGEA and

Below: The outdoor gathering attended by Billy Graham and other delegates to the Berlin Congress on Evangelism, which took place from October 25 to November 1, 1966

Martin Luther King Jr.

Born in 1929, Martin Luther King Jr. was a pastor's son. Originally named Michael King Jr., a family visit to Germany prompted Michael King Sr. to change his and his son's name to Martin Luther King, in honor of the great Reformer. Intellectually gifted, young Martin attended only two years of high school before commencing studies at Morehouse College at the age of fifteen. There he earned a Bachelor of Arts in Sociology, before moving on to Crozer Theological Seminary in Pennsylvania. After graduating in 1951 with Bachelor of Divinity degree, he began doctoral studies in theology at Boston College in Massachusetts, graduating in 1955. Shortly thereafter, King gained national prominence as a leader of the Montgomery Bus Boycott of 1955, a non-violent protest movement that was initiated when a young woman named Rosa Parks was arrested for refusing to give up her bus seat to a white man, as the infamous Jim Crow laws dictated. The boycott lasted 385 days and culminated in a court ruling that ended racial segregation on all Montgomery public buses—but not before King's house was bombed as a result of heightened racial violence.

From this point on, King became the most prominent leader of what came to be known as the Civil Rights Movement. His 'I Have a Dream' speech, given on the steps of the Lincoln Memorial during a march on Washington, D.C. in August 1963, is considered one of the finest and most stirring speeches in American history. In 1964, King was awarded the Nobel Peace Prize. Tragically, just four years later he was assassinated. He was only 39 years old.

Right: Martin Luther King Jr. and Billy Graham.
Dr King credited Graham with doing much to improve race relations in America

Right: *George Washington, America's great general, and some say her greatest president*

Above: *An artist's rending of the U.S. Capitol Building, where some of President Eisenhower's most important speeches were given*

Bottom right: *An artist's rendering of Mount Vernon, the Virginia home of George Washington, the first of many generals to become America's Chief Executive, just as President Eisenhower did*

Christianity Today, the congress had a truly international focus. Papers were delivered charting 'the explosive growth of the church in Africa, Asia and Latin America and the shifting center of gravity of the church from the Western to nonwestern cultures.' Another hallmark was that this concerted effort to bring together Protestant Evangelical Christians from around the world included a diverse amalgam of theologians, evangelists, and church leaders. This led directly to the forging of new relationships, as well as promises of closer cooperation and future gatherings—such as the International Congress on World Evangelization of 1974 (also known as the Lausanne Conference, about which more will be said in the next chapter). Featured speakers included Billy Graham, John Stott, Francis Schaeffer and Corrie Ten Boom.

The statements of these speakers were important to be sure, and produced far-reaching results, but one series of presentations was particularly moving. Just ten years earlier, five American missionaries had been martyred in Ecuador. Now Rachel Saint, widow of one of the five, along with two Waodani tribesmen who had been involved in her husband's murder, was there at the congress. The men shared how they had become Christians through the ministry of Rachel and the other wives who had been widowed. It was an extraordinary example of God's redeeming grace. This story, along with so many of the other stories and presentations that unfolded at the Congress, are now part of the archives of The Billy Graham Center at Wheaton College in Illinois. This treasured collection includes audio recordings, papers and photographs.

Opportunities for fellowship

During the 1950s, Billy Graham had been rebuffed in his efforts to forge a friendship with Reinhold Niebuhr, but this was not the case with two other distinguished theologians Graham had met in August 1960: Karl Barth and Emil Brunner. Graham met Barth and his son Markus not long before a crusade was to be held in Basel, Switzerland. Barth suggested the three climb a mountain, and as they did, Graham told Barth about the forthcoming crusade. 'Don't be disappointed if few people come,' Barth replied in a tone of kindness. 'I believe people will come,' Graham said, 'and at the close of the crusade I will give an invitation to receive Christ.' To

Below: The crusade and its headlines in Little Rock in 1957, two years after racial unrest there. Billy always insisted that 'The ground is level at the foot of the cross.'

Left: Billy Graham and civil rights leader Coretta Scott King, the widow of Martin Luther King, Jr.

this, Barth said he believed few people would respond to such an invitation. When Graham's meeting was held in Basel, 15,000 people came, despite a steady, pouring rain. One of those who attended was Barth himself. Graham preached on the text from John 3:7, 'You must be born again.' It was a night of great blessing, and when he gave the invitation, hundreds came forward. What followed was memorable. Barth and Graham met briefly. 'I agreed largely with your sermon,' the theologian said, 'but I did not like the word *must*. I wish you would change that.' To this Graham replied, 'It's a scriptural word, isn't it?' Barth agreed that it was, but stated that 'one should not give an invitation, one should just declare that God had already acted.' Graham listened, and when his friend finished, he politely disagreed, saying he 'would stick to Scripture.' Looking back on this time, Graham remembered: 'In spite of our theological differences, we remained good friends.'

Graham's visits with Barth set the stage for a sequel of sorts when he met Emil Brunner. During their visit, Graham recounted his conversations with Barth, and when he had finished, Brunner expressed his disagreement with Barth. 'Always put that word *must* in', he said. 'A man *must* be born again'—and, Brunner added, 'I am in favor of the invitation.' All the while, Graham remembered, Brunner was 'warm, friendly and supportive.'

At the President's bedside

On 28 March 1969, former president Dwight D. Eisenhower died. In December 1968, during the final stages of his illness,

Above: *Billy Graham with President and Mrs. Eisenhower. The inscription on this picture, written by the president, reads: 'For Billy Graham, with warm regards from his friend, Dwight Eisenhower'*

he asked Billy Graham to come to his bedside. Though better known for the friendship and pastoral counsel he offered to other presidents, this request for Graham to visit Eisenhower was perhaps the most poignant. Graham had never been able to serve as a chaplain in World War II—something he had dearly wished to do—but when summoned to Eisenhower's bedside, he was able to serve as a chaplain to a man considered by many to be the greatest American soldier of World War II. Graham traveled to the Walter Reed Army Medical Center in Washington, D.C., and that visit was one Graham always considered 'too intimate and sacred' for it to be discussed until after Eisenhower's death. In after years, and with the gracious consent of Mamie Eisenhower, the former president's wife, he told the story of their final visit.

It was a visit that lasted for thirty minutes in all, not the scheduled twenty. General Eisenhower asked the doctor and nurses if they would step outside so that he could speak with Graham alone. The man who had been the picture of strength and resolve during the dark days of World War II was much changed. Propped up on pillows, and receiving medication from intravenous tubes, he grasped Graham's hand. 'Billy,' he said, 'you've told me how to be sure my sins are forgiven and that I'm going to Heaven. Would you tell me again?' At this, Graham took out his ever-present New Testament and read the verses of Scripture that describe all that relates to the promises of God and the hope of eternal life for those who place their faith in Christ. He then prayed a brief prayer for Eisenhower. When he had finished, the former president said: 'Thank you, I'm ready.' That was one of the most moving moments in Graham's pastoral ministry. It was something he would never forget.

A few months later, when Eisenhower died, Graham was asked if he would come to see Mamie Eisenhower. This visit was no less touching than the final visit with the General had been. Graham recalled: 'Mamie welcomed me warmly and asked me to sit beside her. I never understood why she wanted me there just then, instead of a government dignitary or one of her family, but it was an honor to comfort her.' Billy Graham had not had the chance to serve as a chaplain during World War II, but he had been asked by the Eisenhowers to be with them in their hour of need. For a short time, he had been able to be their chaplain. Sometimes that meant just sitting quietly, as he had done with Mamie Eisenhower, and sometimes it meant reaffirming the timeless promises of the gospel and the hope of heaven for the former president. Billy had been allowed to serve as a herald of God's love, and as a trusted friend. These are gifts beyond price.

TRAVEL INFORMATION

The King Center

450 Auburn Ave
Atlanta, GA 30312
www.thekingcenter.org
As its website states, the center was established in 1968 by Coretta Scott King, Dr. King's widow. It is the official, living memorial dedicated to the advancement of the legacy of Martin Luther King, Jr., leader of America's greatest nonviolent movement for justice, equality and peace. More than 650,000 visitors from all over the world are drawn annually to the King Center to pay homage to Dr. King, view unique exhibits illustrating his life and teachings and visit the King Center's Library, Archives, his final resting place, his birth home, gift shop and other facilities. Located in Atlanta's Martin Luther King, Jr. National Historic Site, The King Center utilizes diverse communications media, including books, audio and video cassettes, film, television, CDs and web pages, to reach out far beyond its physical boundaries to educate people all over the world about Dr. King's life, work and his philosophy and methods of nonviolent reconciliation and social change.

Above: *A memorial to Dr Martin Luther King in The King Centre, Atlanta*

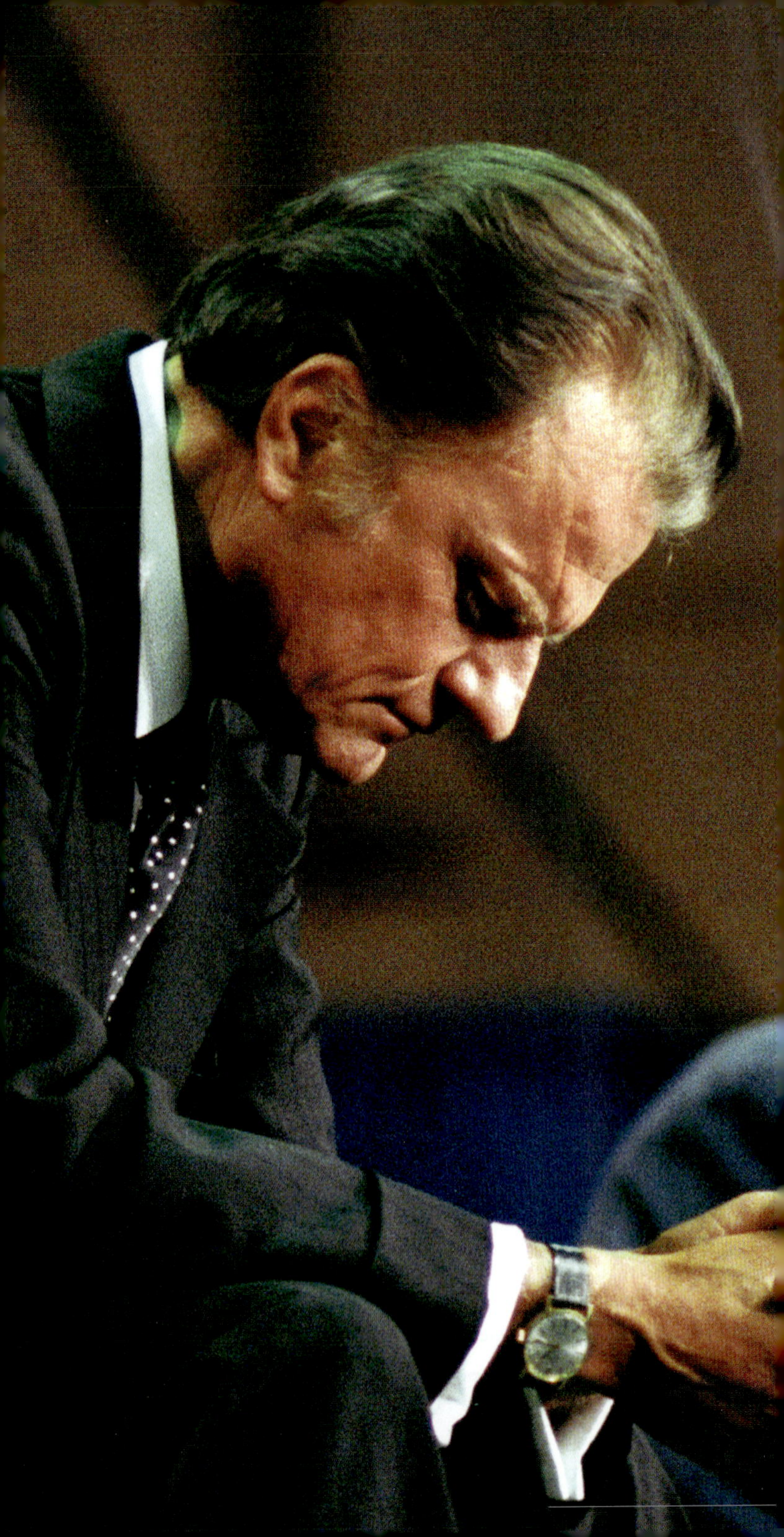

5 The global church

'I have had the privilege of preaching this Gospel on every continent in most of the countries of the world. And I have found that when I present the simple message of the Gospel of Jesus Christ…He takes the message and drives it supernaturally into the human heart'

A hallmark of Billy Graham's ministry in the 1970s was The International Congress on World Evangelization, held at Lausanne, Switzerland in July 1974, or, as it came to be more familiarly known, 'Lausanne '74.' He and his colleagues at the BGEA were very aware of the good that had been done for the spread of the gospel internationally at The World Congress on Evangelism held in Berlin, West Germany from October 25 through November 1, 1966. There was an important spiritual pedigree for both events. The archives of The Billy Graham Center at Wheaton College reveal that The Berlin Congress was 'intended as a spiritual successor of the 1910 World Missionary Conference in Edinburgh, Scotland.' The watchword for the Edinburgh Conference had been 'the evangelization of the world in this generation.' Both the Berlin and Lausanne events wished to carry that watchword and that commitment forward.

The theme of the Lausanne Congress, attended by over 4,000 evangelical leaders from some 150 countries, was 'Let the earth hear His voice.' Held in the Palais de Beaulieu, its intention was to begin the process of dialogue

Facing page: Billy Graham, ardently committed to the power of prayer

Right: A session from Lausanne '74 the profoundly influential congress on world evangelism convened by Billy Graham, John Stott and other Christian leaders of international renown

Above: New College Edinburgh, and the Assembly Hall where the missionary conference was held in 1910

The power of prayer

Prayer has always been central to the ministry of Billy Graham and the BGEA. Indeed, it is the life's-blood of all that has been undertaken for over sixty years. 'I'm convinced,' Billy has said, 'that when Christians of all races and many languages pray for one specific event, God answers. And, in spite of my failures and my crudeness and my limitations, God blesses it and something happens. I believe one of the secrets in our crusades has been this great prayer that has been organized.'

On another occasion, at a minister's breakfast during a preparatory visit to Southern California, Billy warned against false optimism and the belief that 'we can organize spiritual revival…The longer I work in crusades the more convinced I am that salvation is of the Lord. God must prepare hearts.'

Consistently, the BGEA has said that the most effective way people can support its work is to pray for it. This enduring emphasis was powerfully underscored by Billy Graham when he said: 'What a glorious thing it would be if millions of us would avail ourselves of the greatest privilege and the greatest power this side of heaven—the privilege and power of prayer!'

Above: The Lausanne '74 logo—a symbol of a renewed commitment by evangelicals from around the world to global evangelism

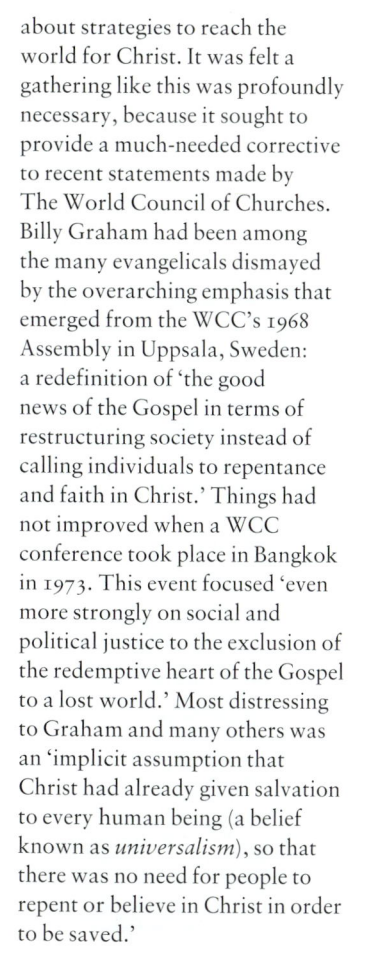

Above: The Palais de Beaulieu, one of the featured venues for the Lausanne International conference

about strategies to reach the world for Christ. It was felt a gathering like this was profoundly necessary, because it sought to provide a much-needed corrective to recent statements made by The World Council of Churches. Billy Graham had been among the many evangelicals dismayed by the overarching emphasis that emerged from the WCC's 1968 Assembly in Uppsala, Sweden: a redefinition of 'the good news of the Gospel in terms of restructuring society instead of calling individuals to repentance and faith in Christ.' Things had not improved when a WCC conference took place in Bangkok in 1973. This event focused 'even more strongly on social and political justice to the exclusion of the redemptive heart of the Gospel to a lost world.' Most distressing to Graham and many others was an 'implicit assumption that Christ had already given salvation to every human being (a belief known as *universalism*), so that there was no need for people to repent or believe in Christ in order to be saved.'

Lausanne '74 was not without controversy. When the writer and BBC presenter Malcolm Muggeridge was placed on the congress program, another scheduled speaker threatened to leave. As Graham remembered, Muggeridge 'was not as well-versed on theological distinctions as this speaker thought he should be. And yet Muggeridge gave a brilliant analysis of the intellectual climate of the world in which we lived.' Many left the congress feeling they had gained a better understanding of how to reach intellectual skeptics for Christ—since they now had a better understanding of the world-view such intellectuals espoused. In his own keynote address, Graham made one unmistakable emphasis: why 'some evangelistic movements of the past had lost their cutting edge.' He maintained that if there is one thing that the history of the church should teach us, it is 'the importance of a theology of evangelism derived from the Scriptures.' His conclusion was stirring: 'Here at Lausanne,

John Stott

Speaking of his great friend John Stott, Billy Graham has said: 'John Stott is the most respected clergyman in the world today.' Indeed, Dr. Stott is best known as an international ambassador for evangelical Christianity. This is the more interesting because, as his online biography states, 'He has lived his whole life within eight blocks of All Souls, the famous central London church he has served for 60 years.' Now Rector Emeritus of All Souls, Dr. Stott has for many years acted faithfully on the charge given him to speak and teach internationally. To that end, the several 'strategic ministry programs' of the Langham Partnership were established. It began in 1969, when Stott founded the Langham Trust. Its purpose was 'to fund scholarships for young evangelical leaders from the Majority World.' Having received the requisite funding, these leaders-in-the-making would 'study at British universities, work toward doctorates in biblical and theological fields, and then return to teach in seminaries in their home countries.'

Dr. Stott's ministry extends also to the many books he has authored. All reflect a high commitment to biblical scholarship, yet they also possess a winsome capacity to speak to the person on the street as well as those who pursue more formal theological training. Dr. Stott's legacy is secure as one who has devoted his life to fostering evangelical Christianity throughout the world. If Billy Graham is regarded as the most prominent preacher of the last half-century, John Stott has had the most prominent and important teaching ministry during this time.

let's make sure evangelization is the one task we are unitedly determined to do.'

Perhaps the most enduring legacy of Lausanne '74 was the document drafted there called the Lausanne Covenant. Each night of the conference, a group of about 40 delegates met to review each line of this document. The English evangelical leader and author, John Stott, was deeply involved in the process though, as Graham states 'he did not write it, as some later assumed.' When this process had concluded, what has come to be known as a classic statement on evangelism had emerged. Graham later assigned particular importance to the paragraph on the nature of evangelism, quoting from it in his autobiography: 'To evangelize is to spread the good news that Jesus Christ died for our sins and was raised from the dead according to the Scriptures, and that as the reigning Lord he now offers the forgiveness of sins and the liberating gift of the Spirit to all who repent and believe… The results of evangelism include obedience to Christ, incorporation into his church and responsible service in the world.'

Corrie Ten Boom

Corrie Ten Boom, a friend of Billy and Ruth Graham alike, was also at Lausanne '74. A survivor of the horrors of the German concentration camps of World War II, this unassuming Dutch lady in her seventies had a testimony that had touched the hearts of tens of thousands around the world. Her witness for Christ was vibrant, powerful and moving. Readers of Corrie Ten Boom's writings in the 1970s will recall her poignant account of the many lovely Christians she met during the days of Lausanne '74. Among the highlights of her time there was her meeting with African Christians from nations ravaged by violence and war. It was with profound sadness she related that when these dear believers returned home, some of them became martyrs for the faith.

Corrie's father and sister had been martyred for their faith when the Nazis arrested and imprisoned them for hiding

Above: *Corrie Ten Boom, heroine of the faith and of the Dutch resistance during World War II. The front cover of her sequel to* The Hiding Place

Left: *Billy Graham and his great friend, John Stott at Montreat, North Carolina, Christmas 1956, with Billy's dog Belshazzar*

Jewish refugees fleeing Hitler's Holocaust pogrom against them. She knew better than most what those African Christians she had met in Lausanne now had to endure. Corrie's story and that of her family was the subject of a widely acclaimed film from World Wide Pictures, the filmmaking ministry of the BGEA. It is perhaps the most compelling of the many fine films produced by this ministry. Highly talented actors and the entire production team combined to make a powerful film which chronicled the witness of one Dutch family that found itself in extraordinary circumstances, their courageous stand for Christ and their deep love for the Jewish people.

During Lausanne '74 Billy Graham had paid tribute to Corrie Ten Boom when he introduced her to the assembled delegates. In a transcript from the congress housed in Wheaton College's archives, he stated: 'Seldom in one's lifetime does one have the privilege of meeting or working with and hearing, a person who is a legend in her own lifetime… Corrie has toured the world, preaching the Gospel of our Lord Jesus Christ, winning many to Christ, by both her writings and her preaching, and now a motion picture has been made on her life, that we think is the finest religious motion picture ever made, and will be in contention, we believe, for an Academy Award this coming year…I want to introduce her today as one of the great women that it's been my privilege to

Above: *The house in Amsterdam where the Ten Boom family lived*

meet.' Her response to Graham's gracious introduction is marked by humility and a deep rootedness in Scripture: 'All [that] you heard has taught me to obey the Lord. [I] pray that you will be strengthened from God's boundless resources, so that you will find yourselves able to plan through any experience, and endure it with courage.'

The premiere of the film called *The Hiding Place* took place in Houston, Texas, on 30 September 1975. A premiere had been planned for the previous day in Hollywood, but it had to be cancelled in the aftermath of a tear-gas attack on the theater by some unknown domestic terrorist. Despite such a frightening reminder of violence *The Hiding Place* and its companion book became highly popular. Many who would not otherwise have heard the gospel

Corrie Ten Boom

Born into a devoutly Christian family in 1892, Corrie Ten Boom lived a relatively quiet life assisting her father as a watchmaker in Haarlem, Holland and devoted much of her free time to local youth organizations. In 1940, Hitler's Nazis invaded Holland and from 1942, Corrie and her family became active in the Dutch underground. Her family's love for the Jewish people was demonstrated time and again as their home became a place of refuge. It was known as 'the hiding place'. Finally, in February 1944, they were betrayed by a Dutch informant and arrested. Corrie's elderly father, Caspar, died in a concentration camp, and while a sister, brother, and nephew were later released, she and her sister Betsie were sent to the Vught political concentration camp and later to the Ravensbruck concentration camp in Germany—infamous for its cruelty. Shortly before her sister Betsie died in September 1944 she had said to Corrie: 'There is no pit so deep that God's love is not deeper still.' Corrie survived her sister, and was released through a 'clerical error' on Christmas Day 1944.

It was now that the second chapter of Corrie's life began. After the war, she began to tell the amazing story of her life and God's work in it. Within a few years, a ministry of international proportions developed. This unassuming heroine of the Holocaust years went on to write many books and lead thousands to Christ. World Wide Pictures, a filmmaking ministry of The Billy Graham Evangelistic Association, produced a film of her life called *The Hiding Place*. It was nominated for the prestigious Golden Globe award in America. In Israel today, her family name is held in great honor, and that is perhaps the most meaningful gift she could ever have received.

The Corrie Ten Boom Museum

19 Barteljorisstraat, in the center of Haarlem, Holland.
www.corrietenboom.com

It addition to chronicling the faith and heroism of the ten Boom family, the museum also includes an exhibition of the Dutch Underground Resistance Movement. Many photographs and mementos of the occupation years are on display.

Above: Billy Graham and World Wide Pictures colleague Dick Ross

heard it through this powerful work of art.

The Hiding Place represented yet another way in which the BGEA ministry team sought to bring the redemptive message of Christ to a needy world. In 1978, a popular television film called *Holocaust* was aired in America. Starring Academy Award winning actress Meryl Streep, the film was later aired in many other places around the world. However, fully three years before, *The Hiding Place* had movingly drawn the world's attention to the Holocaust. It was a visionary ministry as well as a highly effective one—a fitting summary of the BGEA's groundbreaking ministry during the 1970s.

Global evangelism

The words 'the world is my parish' have a famous connection to John Wesley in the 18th century, but they could just as well be viewed as a hallmark of Billy Graham's global evangelistic ministry. His crusades in Africa and Asia stand testament to how vast the territory covered by the BGEA team has been. As if to confirm the sincerity of the Lausanne Conference, the 1970s, for example, was a decade in which Africa and Asia were the focus of many Billy Graham crusades. In 1972, Kohima, Nagaland, India was the site of a crusade. In the following year, 1973, crusades were held in Durban and Johannesburg, South Africa and Seoul, South Korea. In his trips to South Africa, Billy Graham was a prominent opponent of the apartheid system. Missions in China were a way in which Billy and Ruth Graham could visit and share the gospel with people for whom Ruth's family had long felt a great love and burden.

The year 1974 extended the global outreach of the BGEA to South America, with a crusade in Rio de Janeiro, Brazil. 1975 witnessed a return to Asia, with crusades in Taipei, Taiwan and Hong Kong. 1976 marked a return to Africa, with a crusade in Nairobi, Kenya, while 1977 was the year in which a crusade was held in Manila, Philippines—along with a series of Good News Festivals in India. Singapore was the host site for a crusade in 1978, and Sao Paulo, Brazil the host city for a crusade in 1979. In the year 1980, Japan was a country in which four crusades were held, in Okinawa, Osaka, Fukuoka and Tokyo.

This brief overview of the sites the BGEA team visited during the 1970s is more than a snapshot roster of destinations on a map,

Above: *In the King's Park Rugby Stadium, Durban, South Africa in 1973, black and white sat alongside each other*

Above: *With leaders during crusades across the vast continents of Africa and Asia: Prime Minister Indira Gandhi of India (1973), President Boris Yeltsin of The Kremlin, USSR (1991), Prime Minister Jawaharlal Nehru of India (1956), President Kim Il Sung of North Korea (1992) and Prime Minister Golda Meir of Israel (1969).*

it bears eloquent testimony to an enduring commitment. Many evangelistic ministries center their energies on countries in the west, paying scant attention to the crying needs that exist in Africa and Asia. Long before events like the Live Aid concerts of 1985, Billy Graham and his team had a heart for these continents and their people.

A bold and outspoken defender of equality, civil rights and world peace, the Graham crusades were always fully integrated long before the days when this became the norm. It was his firm condition before he would hold a crusade in South Africa during the years of apartheid, and only in 1973 did the South African government relent — his crusades in Johannesburg and Durban reached over 100,000 people and were the first ever integrated public meetings in South Africa. The reason why Billy was always ready to meet with world leaders was not for personal kudos, he saw himself as a peacemaker, taking the words of Christ in Matthew 5:9 seriously 'Blessed are the peacemakers for they shall be called the sons of God.' Wherever he could, he spoke out against violence and the preparations for war. At a Peace Conference in the USSR in May 1982 Billy spoke boldly in defence of religious freedom, and handed to the authorities a list of 150 Christians in prison for their faith. He called upon the leaders of all nations to work for peace 'even when the risks seem high' and on Christians to pray and work for peace 'in whatever constructive ways are open to them' adding 'I do not believe this is only a political issue; it is a moral one as well.'

Nor was he negligent of the tragic and broken areas of the world. He spent Christmas with the troops in Korea in 1952 where he preached at the battlefront, and in Vietnam in 1966 and 1968. He preached in Northern Ireland in 1972 during the troubled days of terrorism.

The world of natural disasters was not forgotten either. He met with the earthquake victims in Guatemala in 1976 and the BGEA chartered ten planes to rush in food and medical supplies. Food was provided for the Bedouins in the deserts and the starving in Senegal, medical supplies for North Korea and remote jungle areas of Kenya, homes and church buildings for Thailand.

The final offering at the Minnesota Crusade in 1973 was for famine relief in Central West Africa. $77,000 was raised at that one meeting and it launched what became the World Emergency Relief Fund. Over the subsequent years this fund has provided food and disaster aid in hundreds of needy areas. When a tidal wave hit Andhra Pradesh in December 1977 Billy, who had been preaching in India, flew directly to see for himself the devastation and to gauge the help needed. Two hundred and eighty five new homes were provided which the people named 'Billy Graham Nagar'. These are only samples of the world-wide compassionate heart of Billy and his team. See page 104 for The Samaritan's Purse.

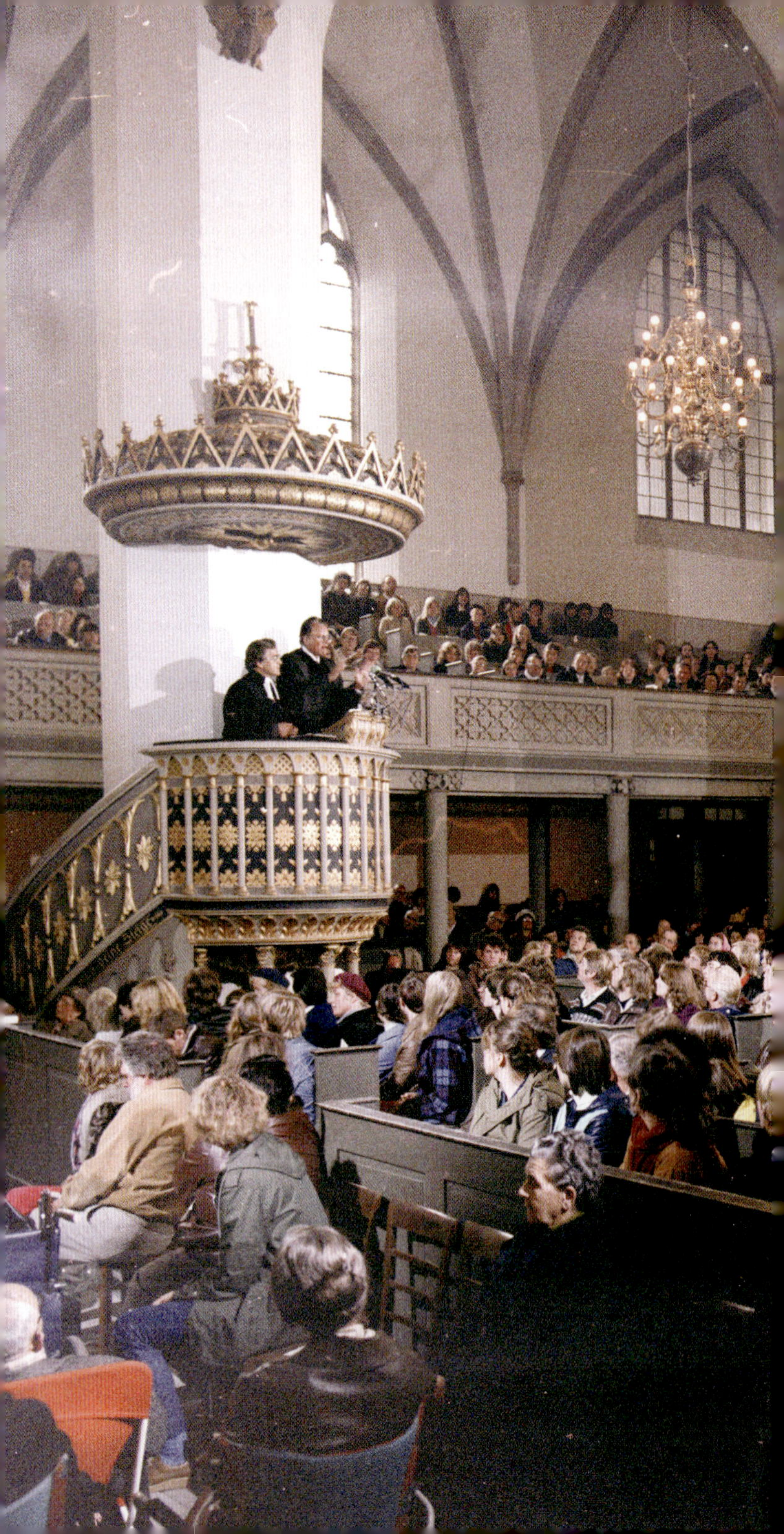

6 Ambassador for Christ

'All that I had been able to do I owe to Jesus Christ. When you honor me you are really honoring him. Any honors I have received I accept with a sense of inadequacy and humility and I will reserve the right to hand all of these someday to Christ, when I see him face-to-face'

If anything, the international scene dominated the 1980s more than it had the 1970s. But sweeping changes were in the air. Billy Graham was close to the epicenter of many key events, including the dawn of the post-communist world. In 1980, much of the world was still caught up in what had come to be called The Cold War. For America, Britain and the Soviet Union, it was the era of détente. Meanwhile, hard economic times were a reality for many in the United States. The final months of Jimmy Carter's presidency were overshadowed by these realities, as they were by the seemingly insoluble hostage crisis in Iran. Billy Graham extended a hand of friendship to President Carter during his administration, as he did to Carter's successor Ronald Reagan. Tragedy very nearly ended Reagan's presidency before it was six months old. An assassin's bullet almost claimed the new President's life on 30 March 1981. For many who watched that awful event unfold on television and prayed the president would survive, it seemed as though a deeply troubled world had suddenly become a darker place still.

To Russia, with love

It was a trying time. And yet, as so often is the case, the most difficult times can be times when God makes a way where there had been none before. It was just a little over a year after the attempt on President Reagan's life, and not long after a series of crusades in New England, that God opened the door for Billy Graham to go to Russia. As envisioned, this visit would be relatively brief, lasting for a week, from 7–13 May 1982. The prospect was met with no little amount of controversy. America's

Facing page: Preaching in East Germany from Martin Luther's pulpit

Right: Billy Graham, with Ronald and Nancy Reagan at the 1969 Anaheim Crusade

ambassador to Moscow, Arthur Hartman, strongly opposed the visit, firmly believing that the Soviet government would use it for propaganda purposes, and many thought Graham naive if he did not see this. By his own admission, Graham was well aware of what the Soviets might try to do: 'Perhaps the Communists in the Soviet Union will try to use me', he told a friend, 'but I'm also going to use them to preach the Gospel.' Considerable pressure mounted as newspapers ran editorials and television networks covered the controversial story. Vice-President George Bush called to express his concerns and read a statement from Ambassador Hartman. However, he stopped short of asking Graham to cancel his trip. Words from President Reagan himself proved the deciding factor. During a dinner at which Graham and Reagans were present, the president took Graham aside and said: 'You know what's been in the press. I believe God works in mysterious ways. I'll be praying for you every mile of the way.'

Much of what Graham was able to do during this trip was little known at the time, but he seized opportunities to exercise what could be called a quiet religious diplomacy. He carried with him a list of prisoners of conscience he believed the Soviets unjustly held, and privately he gave this list to a high-ranking official and expressed his deep concern over the matter. Russian Orthodox and Protestant officials strongly supported his 'behind-the-scenes' approach, though it was little reported by media outlets in the western world.

Preaching in the Moscow Baptist Church and also in the Russian Orthodox Cathedral of

Top: A view of the Kremlin from Moscow's Red Square, a place many thought a Christian leader like Billy Graham would never see—least of all peach there

Left: Billy Graham with the Reagans shortly after their first meeting

Top: Billy Graham preaching in Moscow Baptist Church in 1982

Inset: Billy Graham in the early 1980s with Alexander Dobrynin, longtime Soviet ambassador in Washington, D.C.

the Epiphany, Graham spoke to crowds that had jammed both venues to the walls. He was also able to speak at an international peace conference then being held in Moscow. He told them that the Bible speaks of three kinds of peace: 'peace with God through Jesus Christ, peace within ourselves, and peace with each other. God is concerned about all three aspects, and none is to be ignored if we are to have true peace.' Finally, Graham urged 'all governments to respect the rights of religious believers as outlined in the United Nations Universal Declaration of Human Rights.' That act declared that all governments should 'recognize and respect the freedom of the individual to profess and practice, alone or in community with others, religion or belief, acting in accordance with the dictates of his own conscience.'

The most striking aspect of this visit was as unexpected as it was welcome. It was a visit to Boris Ponomarev, chairman of the Foreign Affairs Committee of the Supreme Soviet of the USSR. Graham had prayed that such a visit might take place—though at the time it seemed the height of impossibility. The most important aspect of this visit concerned the plight of two Siberian Pentecostal families who had sought sanctuary in the American Embassy in Moscow, where they were now living in basement rooms. They wished to emigrate to the United States, but the Soviet government had so far refused to allow this. That

Above: Billy and Ruth with Ronald and Nancy Reagan at the White House. Reagan encouraged Billy Graham to go to Russia since 'God works in mysterious ways'

they had been given sanctuary was a sore subject at present in American-Soviet relations. Graham urged Ponomarev and the Soviet government to find a solution to the problem. He later met privately with the two families at the American Embassy. They were released a year later and allowed to go Israel. Graham had also negotiated permission to meet with Jewish leaders, whose people were being harshly persecuted and denied permission to emigrate from the Soviet Union. Before leaving America, he had met with Rabbi Marc Tanenbaum of the American Jewish Committee

*Right:
Billy Graham greeting an appreciative crowd in Novosibirsk, during his 1984 visit to the Soviet Union*

for a briefing on their plight. Each of these efforts was of a high humanitarian order—and represented the many instances when Billy Graham took a principled stand for human rights.

However, these meetings were overshadowed by the persistent efforts of western journalists to entice Graham to publicly criticize the Soviet government. This he refused to do, in deference to his decision to exercise quiet diplomacy, but it led to charges that he was somehow a communist sympathizer. When, on one occasion, a police escort cleared a busy route so that Graham, who was running late, could reach a destination on time, the press made much of his stopping to thank them—some going so far as to say that he was shaking the hands of police who were persecuting Christians. The idea of Billy Graham being a communist sympathizer was foolish in the extreme, but such charges cast a pall over a visit that in many ways had been important and groundbreaking. In retrospect, this visit should be appreciated

---

Park Street Church, Boston

Located adjacent to Boston Common, and a featured site on the historic Freedom Trail, Park Street Church is one of America's great churches. It was established as an evangelical house of worship and remains true to that heritage of faith today. The site of many historic events, PSC was the place The Handel and Haydn Society of Boston, America's first oratorio society, was organized in 1815. The church was a pioneer in Sunday School education, initiating one of America's first Sunday School programs in 1816. In July 1829, abolitionist William Lloyd Garrison delivered his first anti-slavery address from the Park Street pulpit. PSC holds a revered place in the history of American hymnody as well. Its first organist, Lowell Mason, composed the music for two of Christendom's most beloved hymns: 'Nearer My God to Thee' and 'Joy to the World.'

Moving into the twentieth century, PSC

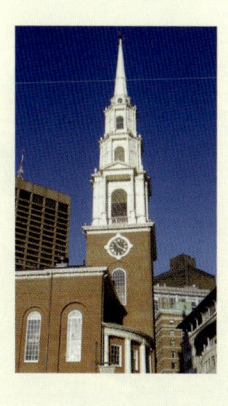

Above: Park Street Church set against the skyline of Boston

continued to develop its innovative and influential ministry. Radio was in its infancy when PSC commenced America's oldest radio ministry in 1923. In 1949, some of the earliest Billy Graham evangelistic crusades were held in Boston at Park Street. PSC's minister in those years, Dr. Harold J. Ockenga, was one of America's most distinguished and accomplished clergymen. He served PSC from 1936 to 1969. He was a co-founder and first President of the National Association of Evangelicals, and was instrumental in the founding of two distinguished seminaries: Fuller Theological Seminary and Gordon-Conwell Theological Seminary.

Center: The Congressional Gold Medal presented to Billy and Ruth Graham in May 1996
Bottom: The Grahams were only the third couple ever to receive this award

for what it was: a first, and if the door of opportunity was opening only part way, it had at least opened. What is more, this trip set the stage for a longer series of visits later in the decade. Sir David Frost once perceptively commented 'Billy Graham has no hidden agendas. He's not an emissary for any government. He's not an emissary for any organization; he is only an emissary for God.'

Recognition and honor

Returning to America at the end of May, Billy and the team undertook what came to be known as the Greater Boston Crusade, which lasted from 30 May through 6 June 1982. It was a chance for Graham and the BGEA team to revisit a part of the United States with which they had close ties, since the former Minister of Boston's Park Street Church, Dr. Harold Ockenga, had been a friend of many years' standing. Here, in old New England, site of the Great Awakening associated with George Whitefield and Jonathan Edwards two centuries

Center: The Presidential Medal of Freedom presented to Billy Graham in 1983
Bottom: Ronald Reagan presenting Billy Graham with the Presidential Medal of Freedom

before, the BGEA team reached thousands for Christ, and strengthened the network of area churches seeking to have a vibrant and effective witness.

Immediately prior to the Greater Boston Crusade, Graham had been accorded a singular honor: the Templeton Foundation Prize for Progress in Religion. Established in 1972 by the late Sir John Templeton, the Templeton Prize 'Honors a living person who has made an exceptional contribution to affirming life's spiritual dimension, whether through insight, discovery, or practical works.' Billy was only the second American to receive the award which has been likened to the Nobel Prize. Other recipients of this prestigious award include Mother Teresa, Russian novelist Aleksandr Solzhenitsyn, Bill Bright, the founder of Campus Crusade for Christ and Charles Colson, the founder of Prison Fellowship. The

Above: Billy Graham with former Prime Minister Margaret Thatcher

presentation ceremony took place in London, England and was awarded by His Royal Highness, Prince Philip. The foundation website reports the following about their decision to make this award: 'When the Rev. Dr. Billy Graham took his message of Christianity into the electronic world of radio and television, he invigorated an entire generation with a simple, yet poignant message of salvation. During his rise as media celebrity, however, he maintained a dignity that continues to draw enormous audiences and enthusiastic support with an interpretation of the Gospel that speaks to the problems and pressures of today.'

In the following year, Graham received another prestigious award in his home country. On 23 February 1983, President Ronald Reagan presented him with the Presidential Medal of Freedom. The citation for this honor read: 'Reverend William "Billy" Graham's untiring evangelism has spread the word of God to every corner of the globe, and made him one of the most inspirational spiritual leaders of the Twentieth Century. As a deeply committed Christian, his challenge to accept Jesus Christ has lifted the hearts, assuaged the sorrows and renewed the hopes of millions. Billy Graham is an American who lives first and always for his fellow citizens. In honoring him, we give thanks for God's greatest spiritual gifts—faith, hope, and love.'

Graham makes only a brief mention of this award in his autobiography. Deeply grateful for the kindness it represented, he commented: 'While he was President, Ronald Reagan bestowed on me one the highest honors I could ever imagine…He presented me with the Presidential Medal of Freedom, the highest civilian honor our government gives to an American, for service to the nation. I felt unworthy of the honor, and still do. But whatever else it means, it will always remind me of the generosity and friendship of a remarkable man and a warm and enduring personal friend.'

Integrity and the family

These marks of recognition underscored the stature Graham now occupied in the Christian world. Such honors meant little to him in the larger scheme of things, and he would always be quick to credit others. Nevertheless, he had become one of the most widely respected ambassadors in the world for the Christian faith. This stemmed from four hallmarks of his ministry: humility, honesty, authenticity and integrity. People are quick to detect sham and pretence—one thinks of how hard hitting interviewers like David Frost could be with those he thought guilty of both as his interviews with former President Richard Nixon attest. But in Graham's interviews with Frost, Billy would readily admit mistakes, discuss things he wished he had done differently or say that like all of us he struggled at times with temptation. A Kirkus review of the book *Billy Graham in Conversation* contains the following reflection from Frost: '[Graham's] secret appears to lie in his simple, boiled-down faith. In his own words, he is refreshingly straightforward: "The message that the world needs and is hungering for is that God is. People today are hungry to know about God and it is wonderful when they hear that God loves them, He is a person and He is willing to forgive them."' There was, Frost

Above: *One of the several occasions Billy has met Queen Elizabeth II, pictured together with the late Queen Mother and Duke of Edinburgh*

Below: *With former President Jimmy Carter*

had detected, a winsomeness about Graham's honesty in discussing 'politics, pain and suffering, presidents, sin and temptation.'

It was once said that a major reason why Prime Minister William Pitt cherished his friendship with William Wilberforce was that Pitt knew Wilberforce would never ask any self-serving favors of him. Graham carried himself in a similar way with world leaders, or those aspiring to become one. During the 1980 presidential campaign, Ronald Reagan, a friend of long standing, asked Graham to release a positive public statement about him. Graham's reply was revealing: 'Ron, I can't do that. You and I have been friends for a long time, and I have great confidence in you. I believe you are going to win the nomination and be elected President. But I think it would hurt us both, and certainly hurt my ministry, if I publicly endorsed any candidate.' Graham had no sooner said this to Reagan than he was asked by one of Reagan's aides if he would accompany the candidate to church. 'I can't do that,' Graham said apologetically. 'If I were to go with you now, it would be perceived as an endorsement. I just can't do it.' The aide, Graham later recalled, 'looked peeved, but I nonetheless thought that he understood my concern to be strictly neutral in the political race, in spite of my friendship with the Reagans.'

Friendships have been shipwrecked for less; and there was a cost-counting aspect to such a principled stand. But the preservation of a ministry's integrity was always Billy's primary concern. Many a clergyman has fancied himself as a kingmaker, or sought to be; but always, such a practice has tarnished the person's ministry and diminished future opportunities for ministry. Through hard-won personal experience, Graham had come to understand that leaders of all parties needed to feel that they could seek pastoral counsel from him. By his own actions, he would not exclude anyone from hearing the life-changing message of Christ. To do so would be wrong.

The world's press is always ready to catch any moral lapse in those within its sights, but however hard they tried, they failed totally to pin anything onto Billy Graham. His relationship with his wife and family has proved to be a model of Christian love, commitment and purity. *Time* magazine for Monday 14 June 1999 ran an article on 'The World's 100 Most Influential

Above: The children at home with Ruth in 1958

Above: *Ruth and Billy on their fiftieth wedding anniversary in 1993 at their home with the family in Montreat*

People'. Harold Bloom focussed on Billy Graham and concluded: 'There have been no scandals, financial or sexual, to darken Graham's mission. His sincerity, transparent and convincing, cannot be denied.' To the charge that he must have made a fortune from his fame, considering the high costs of the crusades and his successful book sales, the facts speak for themselves. In an article in *The New York Times* for 3 February 1993 entitled: 'America's Pastor', Peter Steinfels concluded: 'Likewise, Mr. Graham long ago put himself on a fixed salary, now $80,000 a year, while the highly efficient Billy Graham Evangelistic Association, overseen by outsiders, handles millions of dollars used in its operations. Most of his book royalties go back to the ministry or to charity.' We can add to this the fact that the $200,000 cheque he received in 1982 as the Templeton Foundation Prize he donated immediately to world relief, the training of evangelists in developing countries, and evangelism in Britain. More than a half century of public ministry in the searching spotlight of the world's press and paparazzi has left this global ambassador for Christ and the gospel without a stain on his character or reputation.

In the home, Billy was consistent as a husband and father. The finest testimony must surely come from those who know him best. Gigi, the eldest daughter of Billy and Ruth, has commended: 'Because of their example, I respected them and listened to their advice. I saw Daddy live what he preached. I saw them making Christ their life—not just their religion.' The love that Ruth and Billy shared for more than half a century grew with the passing years and Billy could claim that he loved his wife even more at the end than at the beginning. For all his busyness as a global evangelist, and the many weeks he had to spend away from home, it was always his greatest joy to return to the comfort, security, privacy and love that Ruth provided in their mountaintop home in the Appalachian hills. As the family grew and left home, the relationships stayed firm. Billy advises: 'The same principles and promises we applied to our children are still true for our grandchildren and great-grandchildren. We pray for each one each day and spend time on weekends talking with them on the phone.' Throughout his long and demanding ministry, Billy always had time for his children; they knew what it was to play with their daddy and for him to weep with them in their times of need. But 'without Mother', daughter Ruth concedes, 'Daddy's ministry would not have been possible.' Ruth's commitment to her husband's work has already been referred to (see page 19). They have made a wonderful partnership and provide a model of a true Christian marriage. This, no less than the wide public preaching of Billy Graham, is a great part of their legacy today.

TRAVEL INFORMATION

Park Street Church, Boston

One Park Street
Boston, MA 02108
617–523–3383
email: info@parkstreet.org
www.parkstreet.org

Boston's Freedom Trail, as its website states (www.thefreedomtrail.org) it is a walking trail in which visitors to Boston can take in the rich history of America's Revolution (1775–1783)—the events that lead up to the historic break from Britain and the brave people who shaped America's national government. The trail itself is a 2.5 mile red-brick walking trail that leads you to 16 nationally significant historic sites, every one an authentic American treasure. Preserved and dedicated by the citizens of Boston in 1958, when the wrecking ball threatened, the Freedom Trail today is a unique collection of museums, churches, meeting houses, burying grounds, parks, a ship, and historic markers that tell the story of the American Revolution and beyond. www.thefreedomtrail.org/maps/maps.html

CHRIST CHURCH, SALEM STREET.

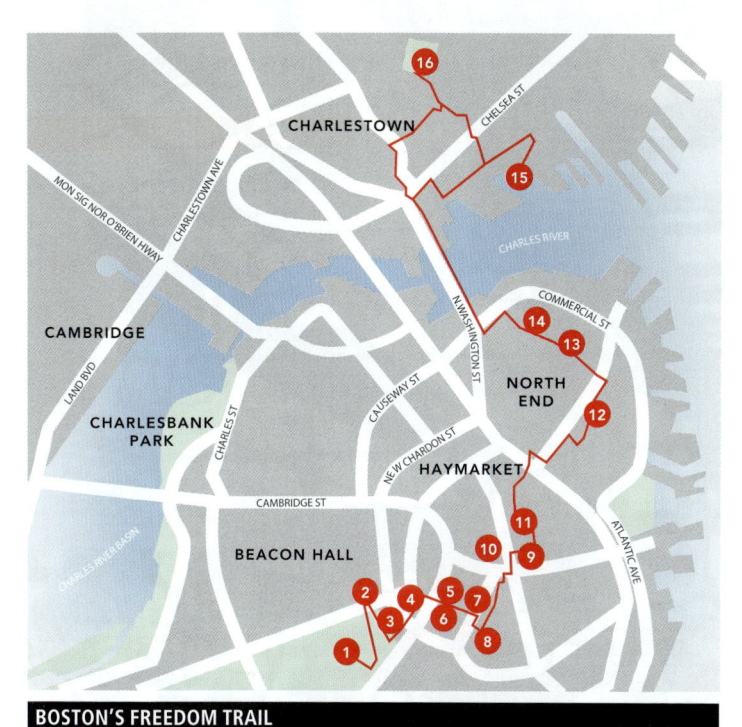

BOSTON'S FREEDOM TRAIL

1 Boston Common
2 State House
3 Park Street Church
4 Granary Burying Ground
5 King's Chapel and Burying Ground
6 First Public School Site
7 Old Corner Bookstore
8 Old South Meeting House
9 Old State House
10 Boston Massacre Site
11 Faneuil Hall
12 Paul Revere House
13 Old North Church
14 Copp's Hill Burying Ground
15 USS Constitution
16 Bunker Hill Monument

What to see on the Freedom Trail

People often like to start their trek along the Freedom Trail at the Boston Common—one of America's most beautiful inner-city parks. Along the way, trail walkers can see the Bunker Hill Monument, King's Chapel, Park Street Church, the Old Corner Bookstore, the Benjamin Franklin statue and original site of America's first public school, the Boston Latin School, the U.S.S. Constitution, Faneuil Hall, the Old North Church, the Paul Revere House, the Old South Meeting House and the Old State House. Other stops along the trail include the Granary Burying Ground, the King's Chapel Burying Ground and the Copp's Hill Burying Ground. Visitors should also note that The Black Heritage Trail crosses the Freedom Trail between the Massachusetts State House and Park Street Church.

Opposite: Christ Church, or, as it is more commonly known, the Old North Church, a famous site on Boston's Freedom Trail

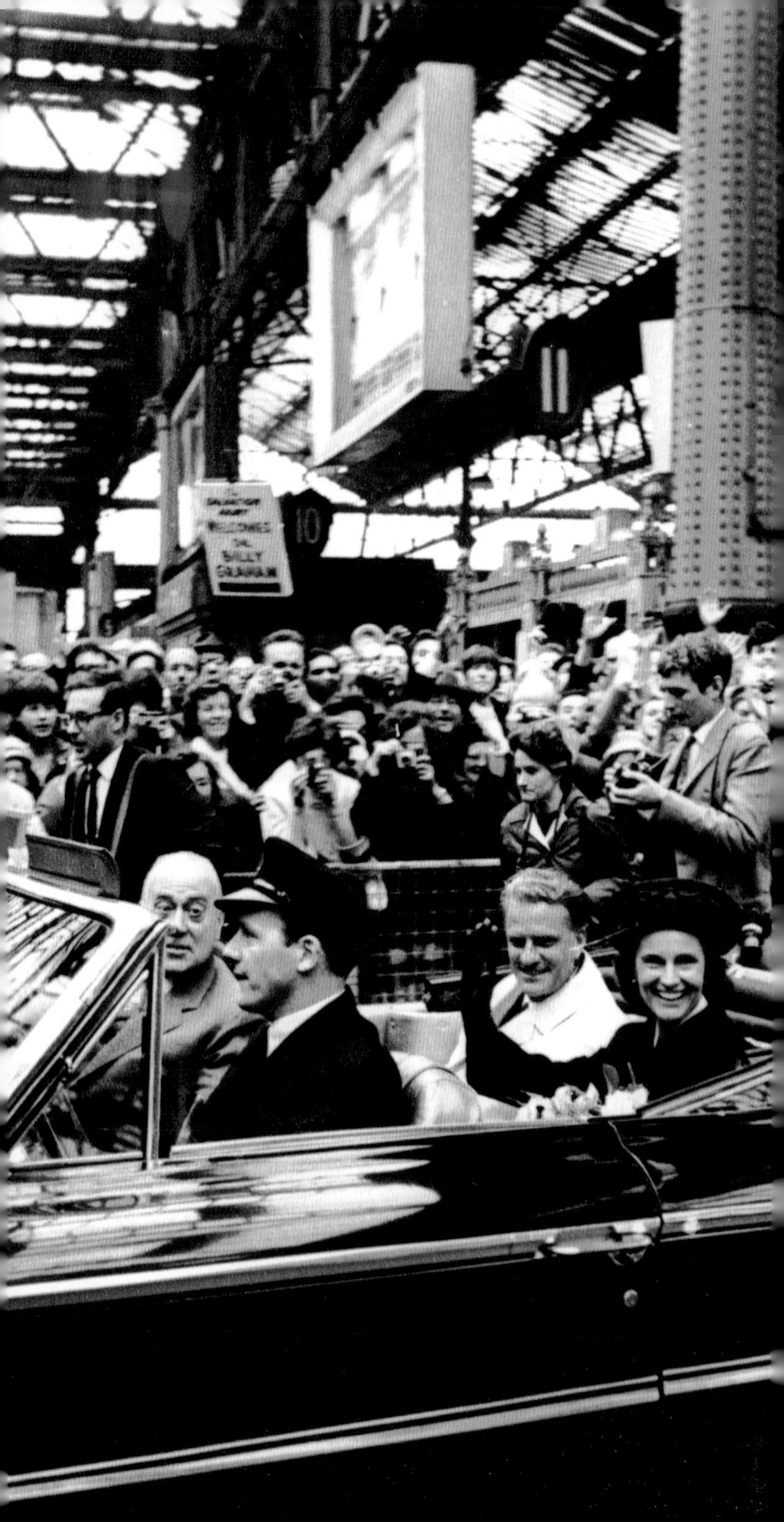

⑦ Passing the mantle

'I present a God who matters, and who makes claims on the human race. He is a God of love, grace and mercy, but also a God of judgment. When we break His moral laws we suffer; when we keep them we have inward peace and joy'

On 1 June 1966 the BGEA's 32-day Greater London Crusade began. It was a series of events that left a lasting impression. Huge billboards with a picture of Billy preaching and the simple strapline: 'Worth listening to' faced Londoners everywhere. Dennis Robson, an Assemblies of God pastor, was one of the drivers for Billy and Ruth Graham during the six weeks of this crusade. Dennis met them for the first time at Waterloo Station when they arrived on the boat train. It was quite a scene, as hundreds of hymn singing Christians greeted their arrival. He was not used to driving a car with an automatic transmission, and when he pressed the car's 'non-existent clutch' upon arriving at the Graham's hotel, it caused Billy and Ruth 'to rise to their feet in the back of the open top Ford Galaxy in full view of the welcome party!' Greatly embarrassed, Dennis was however impressed by the fact that the Grahams didn't seem to mind. More of what made Billy Graham special surfaced when he discovered that Dennis (and his fellow driver Ray) were really pastors. Billy insisted that they no longer wear their bogus chauffeur's caps! Over time, Dennis learned that Billy preferred being driven by

Facing page:
Billy and Ruth Graham, en route to the Earls Court Crusade of 1966

Right: Three young men who were Billy's drivers for the 1966 crusade in England. From left: Ray Westbrook, Peter Friday and Dennis Robson

Christian men, as this allowed him to relax more in the back of the car after the services. When Billy returned to London the following year for a week of meetings in the Royal Albert Hall, he specially asked for Dennis to chauffeur him again. Dennis (and Ray) always found Billy to be appreciative and considerate. He was, Dennis remembered, 'a very humble, gentle man.' He was no less impressed with the kindness he was shown by Ruth Graham. On one occasion, when she returned from a visit to America, she gave Dennis a dress for his baby daughter. It has become a family treasure.

Dennis recalls that after meeting the Queen in Buckingham palace Billy Graham commented, 'I always talk to everyone about Jesus. If I didn't, the Lord would not give me future opportunities.' One reporter asked Billy how he felt when he met the Royal Family. He replied that it was 'a great privilege.' but 'it was a greater one to preach before the King of kings every day.'

Another driver for the Earls Court Crusade was the then 21-year-old Peter Friday, who remembers the enjoyment of experiencing a 'weekend away' with Billy and Ruth Graham. Together they travelled to Oxford, attended a Sunday morning service, and drove on to Cambridge for an evening meeting. Peter recalls that when they stopped off for their roadside picnic, Ruth Graham put on a scarf and dark glasses as a disguise so not to be recognized by passing traffic!' The kindness and thoughtfulness of the Grahams are what lingers in his mind: 'After parking the car,

Above: *Years later Dennis and Ray, who were both pastors with the Assemblies of God, met with Billy at a reception in the late 1980s*

Left: Billy and Ruth Graham, being greeted by well-wishers on the eve of the Earls Court Crusade 24 May 1966

Earls Court Exhibition Centre

One of the most notable places in the U.K. where Billy Graham has spoken is the Earls Court Exhibition Centre. Located in West London, it is a premier exhibition centre and entertainment venue. It is in fact the second largest exhibition centre in London. Patrons may arrive for scheduled events via two underground stations, Earls Court and West Brompton. The site of many music concerts, Earls Court is also the site for award ceremonies, among them the BRIT Awards. It is also home to the Ideal Home Exhibition and the MPH show—one of Britain's largest motoring exhibitions and shows. A summer highlight at Earls Court for many years (1950–1999) was the Royal Tournament, described as 'the first, oldest and biggest military tattoo in the world.'

Earls Court has continued to grow as an exhibition and entertainment site, so much so that another huge building, Earls Court Two, was constructed at considerable cost where the Lillie Bridge was once located. A marvel of civil engineering, Earls Court Two boasts a striking barrel-roofed hall that provides a column-free 17,000 square metre floor—to this day Europe's biggest unsupported roof span. It links with Earls Court One by way of a system of folding shutters. Earls Court Two was opened by Diana, Princess of Wales on 17 October 1991. Earls Court One opened for business in 1937.

In the past, other shows held at the Earls Court site have included the London Boat Show, the British Motor Show, the London Book Fair and the Good Food Show. The future for this venue continues to look bright, as it has been announced that during the 2012 Olympics, Earls Court will be the host site for the volleyball competitions.

Wembley Stadium —the pride of northwest London

Wembley Stadium is as beloved a sports venue as there is in the world. Known as 'the home of football,' this newly renovated facility with a one kilometer circumference seats 90,000 and is the largest stadium in the world with every seat under cover. The England national football team is the primary user of Wembley Stadium, but it has played host to many other celebrated concerts and sporting events. It was the site of a World Cup final in 1995, and of a ten-year anniversary memorial concert for Diana, Princess of Wales. But the history of sport at Wembley goes back much further. As early as the 1880s, when the site was known as the Wembley Leisure Park Grounds, football and cricket pitches, as well as a running track, were to be found there. Following the end of the Great War in 1918, the British government began planning a British Empire Exhibition. The Wembley Park Leisure Ground was selected as the best site to construct a National Sports Ground. The first sporting event at the 'Empire Stadium,' as it was then called, was the famous 'White Horse Cup Final' of 1923 in which Bolton beat West Ham. The following year it hosted the British Empire Exhibition, and in 1948 the 14th Olympic Games. The stadium, which originally had a capacity of 120,000, was demolished in 2003 and four years later the new stadium was opened under the name 'new Wembley Stadium'. It is the host not only of sporting events but major musical concerts. It will be a significant centre for the London 2012 Olympics. On several occasions Wembley Stadium has been the site for crusade events led by Billy Graham, most notably in 1954 when the climax of the Crusade saw an estimated 120,000 squeezing into the stadium with a further 67,000 in the nearby White City Stadium. Crusade meetings were also held at Wembley on many ocassions from 1955.
See also page 105.

Above: Wembley Stadium hosting the 1966 London Crusade, where a capacity 95,000 listened to Billy Graham in the stadium with another 8,000 outside

Above: Advances in technology like satellite broadcasting have meant that the message of the gospel can reach more people than ever before—sometimes in many countries simultaneously

I was welcomed at the table with the guests and treated like one of the family…My long lasting impression will always be Billy Graham's humility. It was a privilege to drive the Grahams and their team members, and to feel at one with them.'

This crusade in 1966 was remembered for its prayer backing across the United Kingdom. It is estimated that nine thousand 'cottage prayer meetings' were eventually established across the nation, organised by Jenny, the wife of evangelist Tom Rees. Billy and Ruth arrived at Southampton from the liner Queen Mary and took the boat train to Waterloo where thousands greeted the American Baptist preacher. Over 90,000 packed into Wembly Stadium, and thousands responded to the call to repentance and faith in Christ. So successful was this crusade that Billy was back in London a year later.

As in all the Graham Crusades, his three drivers were only a few of the army of volunteers that made the crusades possible by their time and skill so freely given. Thousands of Christians are involved in forming prayer groups, planning, stewarding, counselling, singing in the choir, follow-up of enquirers. The organization is a blend of business-like efficiency and total dependence upon God.

A global electronic pulpit and the printed page

On 1 June 1957 the New York Crusade at Madison Square

Left: Billy Graham writing and revising in earlier years with his personal assistant, T W Wilson

Below: The front cover of Just As I Am, *Billy Graham's long-awaited autobiography, published in 1997*

Opposite left: The front cover of Billy's first book published in 1953

Opposite right: Perhaps his most successful book of all which sold one million copies in its first three months

Garden opened, and its Saturday meetings were telecast for one hour on the ABC television network; this continued at prime time for seventeen weeks. But that was merely a beginning. In 1989, Billy Graham preached from London to more than 800,000 people by means of 247 'live-link' centers throughout the United Kingdom and the Republic of Ireland. This broadcast was also heard at 16,000 sites among thirteen nations of Africa. Other numbers associated with this innovative use of technology were also significant. Another twenty African nations received videotaped copies of the broadcast within two weeks of the event. This allowed for translation into one of nine different languages. It was estimated that the aggregate attendance at the African sites exceeded eight million people. In November 1990, technology similar to that used for the London event was used to beam Dr. Graham's sermons from Hong Kong to an estimated 100 million souls assembled at 70,000 locations in twenty-six countries of Asia.

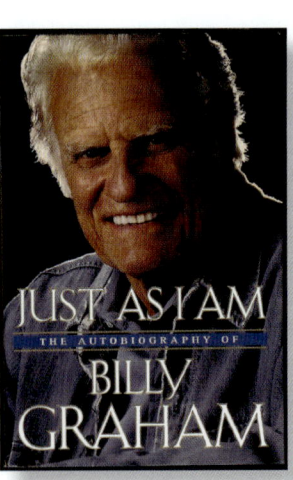

The London and Hong Kong events demonstrated the extent to which Billy Graham was now preaching from a global electronic pulpit. He and his associates at the BGEA embraced the use of these new technological advances as a means of greater stewardship and effectiveness in proclaiming the gospel. An incredible amount of hard work and innovative thinking were required to make this new means of 'going into all the world' a success. There were many technological challenges to overcome, but the results were worth all the labor expended.

Another very labor-intensive project for the BGEA was the preparation and writing of Billy Graham's long-awaited autobiography. In 1991, William Martin had published a 735-page biography entitled *A Prophet with Honor: The Billy Graham Story*.

task took ten years. Among the many challenges associated with this undertaking were carving out time from an incredibly busy schedule to write, and assembling a team of editors and researchers. Why undertake such a daunting task? Two or three insights proved to be the deciding factors: 'I thought of the next generation', Graham wrote, 'who might be encouraged by such a book to believe that God can do in their generation what He did in ours.' Secondly, 'I came to see that in its own way this book could be a ministry also.' A third insight came from the counsel of his colleagues, who encouraged Billy

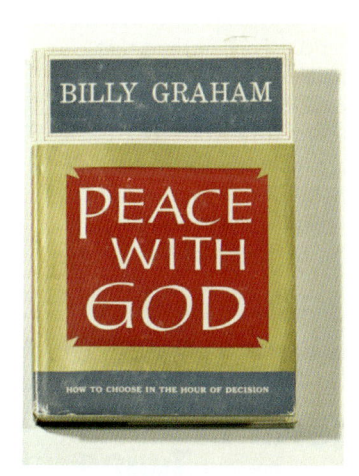

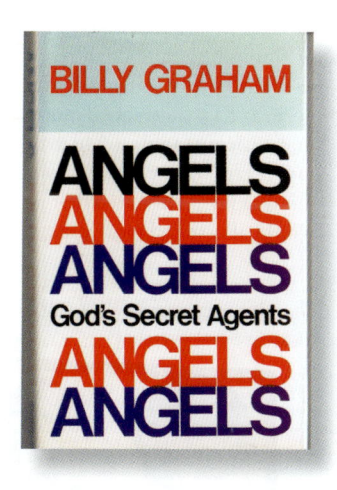

The book was well received, but for many it only whetted their appetite to hear Graham tell his life story in his own words. How he came to do that proved to be a gradual process. 'To be honest,' he stated in the Preface to *Just As I Am*, 'I never thought I would write this book.' In the end, the

with the thought that 'there were lessons to be learned from the ministry God had entrusted to us.'

And so, in 1997, the respected publishing company HarperCollins published *Just As I Am*. It is a remarkable book with many virtues. It does indeed tell the stories of how God's work unfolded in Billy Graham's life, and in the lives of so many others, in a way that only he could tell them. Reviewers have noted many of the book's distinguishing characteristics—its honesty, humor and charitable spirit. Added to these traits are humility and self-criticism. 'I have much to be grateful for as I look back over my life', Graham affirmed, but 'I also have many regrets. I have failed many times, and I would do many things differently.' What then unfolded was a series of admissions and reflections, displaying the kind of candor that has earned the respect of seasoned journalists like Sir David Frost.

Near the close of *Just As I Am*, the evangelist wrote that among the things he would do differently he 'would speak less and study more, and I would spend more time with my family…Much of [my] travel was necessary, some of it was not.' He stated that he 'would also spend more time in spiritual nurture, seeking to grow closer to God… And I would give more attention to fellowship with other Christians, who could teach me and encourage me (and even rebuke me when necessary).' He continued: 'If I had it to do all over again, I would also avoid any semblance of involvement in partisan politics … there have been times when I undoubtedly stepped over the line between politics and my calling as an evangelist…Becoming involved in strictly political issues or partisan politics inevitably dilutes the evangelist's impact and compromises his message. It is a lesson I wish I had learned earlier.'

At the same time, Graham reflected on one thing that had impressed him powerfully over his decades of travel and evangelistic work: 'I have crossed paths with people who hold virtually every kind of religious and philosophical view

Above: *Ticket for a crusade conducted jointly in 1998 by Billy and Franklin Graham*

Above: Father and son during the 1970s

imaginable. Often I am moved by the intensity of their spiritual searching… At the same time, as the years have gone by, I myself have become even more convinced of the uniqueness and truth of the Gospel of Christ.' Such deep sympathy for those who are searching, combined with a steadfast commitment to holding forth the gospel, has distinguished Graham's ministry. In countless ways, he has sought to come alongside those who are searching, inviting them to join him on the path of Christian pilgrimage.

Billy's first book, *Peace with God*, was written out of the deep conviction that 'a book presenting the Gospel in a simple but comprehensive way, was what people who had little or no religious background needed.' Published in 1953, millions of copies in fifty languages were eventually published. Of his twenty titles published, perhaps Billy Graham's book on *Angels* was his most immediately successful — it sold one million copies in three months and within fifteen months it had sold more copies in hardback than any other book in American history! Almost all the royalties from his books are donated to charitable causes.

Father and son

Even as he had always invited seekers to join him on the path of pilgrimage, health problems now meant that Billy Graham would have to ask a successor to join him on the path of ministry. By 1995, the symptoms of Parkinson's disease had become pronounced. Graham would be able to continue in ministry, hopefully for many more years yet, but thought had to be given to a successor. The solution could not have been more gratifying. The board of the BGEA decided that Franklin Graham, the evangelist's eldest son, would fill this role.

Franklin's younger years had been more than a little disturbing to his parents, with incidents of carousing and school expulsions. He smoked, drank, got into fights and tried marijuana. He drove a motorcycle fast, living for the adrenaline rush. Being the eldest son of so famous a father was not easy, and there were many times when that reality sat uncomfortably on his shoulders. But all this changed in 1974 when father and son were together in Switzerland. Billy had a sobering, heartfelt talk with his 22-year-old son. The story is recounted

Left: Father and son during a crusade in the 1990s

in Franklin's autobiography *Rebel with a Cause: Finally Comfortable Being Graham*. Franklin remembered his father looking him in the eye and saying, 'I want you to know that your mother and I sense there is a struggle for the soul of your life, and you're going to have to make a choice.'

Father and son parted after that conversation, and the younger Graham continued on a driving tour of Europe, a bottle of Scotch to hand. But he could not stop thinking about what his father had said. It was in a hotel room in Jerusalem that Franklin's life changed. 'That night,' he wrote, 'instead of going to the bar for a couple of beers, I found myself alone in my room reading through the gospel of John. When I came to the third chapter, I read not just that Jesus told Nicodemus he had to be born again, but I also grasped that Franklin Graham had to be

Above: *Franklin Graham to whom Billy Graham passed the mantle of ministry*

Above: *Franklin Graham delivering the invocation at President Bush's Second Inauguration*

born again as well.' Not long afterward, Franklin returned to his family's home in North Carolina. There he married a hometown girl, Jane Austin Cunningham, and during the ceremony on his parents' front lawn he publicly told everyone how his life had changed.

At first, Franklin was reluctant to preach, and shortly after this conversion he became active in the leadership of the Christian relief organization Samaritan's Purse. In 1979, one year after the death of its founder and family friend Bob Pierce, Franklin took over as president and chairman. Ever since that time, Samaritan's Purse has helped millions of people around the world. It could not have been more gratifying to Billy Graham to have his son assume his mantle in ministry. Franklin had learned what it was to lead a large organization, and face the many challenges that brings with it.

However, he also discovered his own gift for preaching, and Franklin held his first solo crusade in 1989 in Alaska. He quickly changed the name 'crusade' to 'festival' in recognition of the need to attract a younger generation, and he added music from Christian artists. In the year 2000, the Board of BGEA unanimously appointed Franklin as his father's heir to the ministry. A gifted preacher and evangelist, Franklin continues to conduct crusades world wide, and during the last two months of 2007 he preached at the Hong Kong Franklin Graham Festival. This was the first major evangelistic crusade in Hong Kong since it came under communist rule in 1997 — and more than 420,000 attended. Father and son could now work together in concert.

Samaritan's Purse

Since Franklin Graham assumed leadership of Samaritan's Purse in 1979, the organization's annual budget has grown from approximately $500,000 to more than $250 million. In 2005, Samaritan's Purse provided aid and relief services to underprivileged people in more than 140 countries around the world.

The website for Samaritan's Purse (www.samaritanspurse.org) says this about its mission: 'For over 35 years, Samaritan's Purse has done our utmost to follow Christ's command by going to the aid of the world's poor, sick, and suffering. We are an effective means of reaching hurting people in countries around the world with food, medicine, and other assistance in the Name of Jesus Christ. This, in turn, earns us a hearing for the Gospel, the Good News of eternal life through Jesus Christ. Our emergency relief programs provide desperately needed assistance to victims of natural disaster, war, disease, and famine. As we offer food, water, and temporary shelter, we meet critical needs and give people a chance to rebuild their lives. Our community development and vocational programs in impoverished villages and neighborhoods help people break the cycle of poverty and give them hope for a better tomorrow. We impact the lives of vulnerable children through educational, feeding, clothing, and shelter programs that let them know they are not forgotten. We provide first-class treatment in the Name of the Great Physician through our medical projects, as well as supplying mission hospitals with much needed equipment and supplies.' Samaritan's Purse was launched in the UK in May 1990 and in 1995 Operation Christmas Child merged with Samaritan's Purse. Each year more than four million shoe boxes, filled with goodies, are delivered to needy children in eighty-six countries across the world.

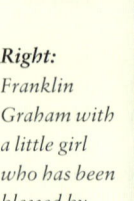

Above: Billy Graham and Franklin Graham distributing food at a Samaritan's Purse Thanksgiving Day event

Right: Franklin Graham with a little girl who has been blessed by Samaritan's Purse

TRAVEL INFORMATION

Wembley Stadium

London, HA9 0WS
To visit the website for Wembley Stadium, and to learn about its history and options for a tour, go to:
www.wembleystadium.com

What to do in and around Wembley

Visitors to Wembley Stadium are in close proximity to several sites well worth visiting. One may take a tour of the **BBC Television Centre**. Its address is:
BBC Television Centre,
Hammersmith and Fulham, W12 7RJ

The nearest tube stations are: Wood Lane Underground Station (0.1 km) and White City Tube Station (0.2 km). The nearest rail station is Shepherds Bush Station (Overground, 0.7 km).

Those who appreciate the fine arts can visit **The Ben Uri Art Gallery** of London Jewish Museum of Art.
108a Boundary Road,
Camden, NW8 0RH

For directions on how to visit this cultural center, go to: www.visitlondon.com/attractions/detail/281377
Those who welcome a walk in the park can visit **Aldenham Country Park**.
Hertsmere, Borehamwood, WD6 3AT
For directions to visit this park, go to:
www.visitlondon.com/attractions/detail/266171

Those who frequent museums can visit one of the world's best, **The Victoria and Albert Museum**. Its address is:
Cromwell Road,
Kensington and Chelsea, SW7 2RL

The nearest tube station is South Kensington, served by the District, Circle and Piccadilly lines. On the District and Circle lines the station is between Gloucester Road and Sloane Square, and on the Piccadilly Line it is between Gloucester Road and Knightsbridge. South Kensington is the easternmost interchange between these three lines; the Circle and District lines diverge from the Piccadilly line slightly east of the station. It is in Travelcard Zone 1

The main station entrance is located at the junction of Old Brompton Road (A3218), Thurlow Place, Harrington Road, Onslow Place and Pelham Street. Subsidiary entrances are located in Exhibition Road giving access by pedestrian tunnel to the **Natural History**, **Science** and **Victoria and Albert Museums**.
Also close by are **Imperial College London** and the **Royal College of Music**.

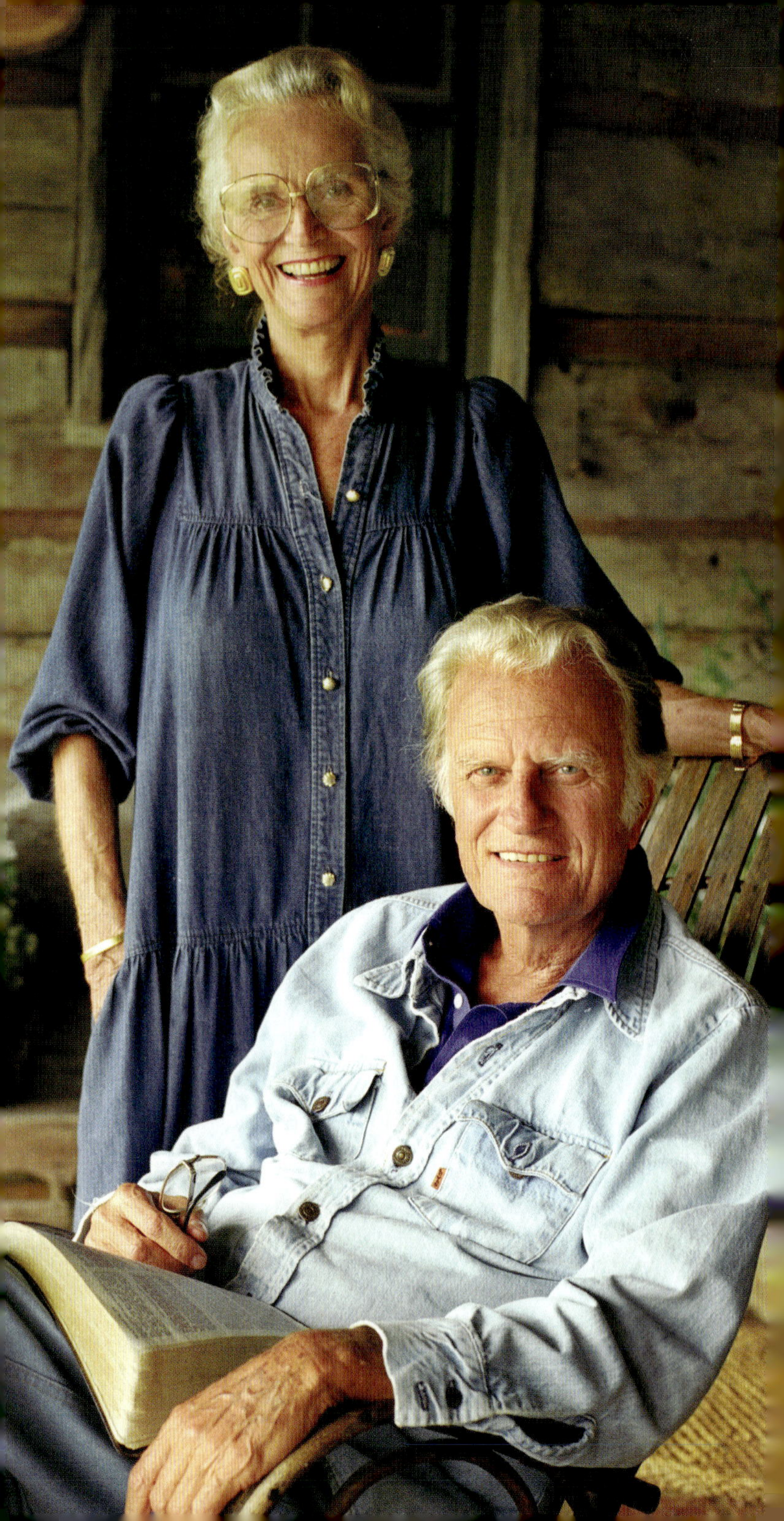

8 The lasting legacy

'I realize that my ministry would someday come to an end. I am only one in a glorious chain of men and women God has raised up through the centuries to build Christ's Church and to take the Gospel everywhere'

For Billy Graham, the years of the twenty-first century have been the evening of his life. The last decade has seen times of tragedy, and times of milestones and goodbyes. This time has also marked the close of Dr. Graham's active evangelistic ministry. At the dawn of the twenty first century, the Billy Graham Evangelistic Association entered its sixth decade of ministry. Yet scarcely had this new century begun when tragedy struck. A series of terrorist attacks on 11 September 2001 shocked America and nations throughout the globe. For many it seemed as though the world would never be quite the same again.

The nation's pastor

As Americans struggled to come to terms with what had happened, a service at Washington's National Cathedral was scheduled for September 14th. Billy Graham was asked to give a message during this time of national mourning. As he made his way to the pulpit, frail but purposeful, many were reminded anew why so many consider Billy Graham to be America's pastor. As the camera panned out over those assembled in the cathedral, it seemed as though every statesman or dignitary from among America's leaders, as well as leaders of many other nations were there. Leaders and dignitaries they may have been, but for that day they—and the millions who watched the service on television—were united

Above: Billy Graham speaking at the National Cathedral in Washington on the Day of Remembrance following the terrorist attacks on 11 September 2001

Facing page: Billy and Ruth Graham—life partners, a blessing to millions

Above: *President and Mrs. Bush taking part in the service at the National Cathedral in Washington on the Day of Remembrance following the terrorist attacks on 11 September 2001*

in their sense of collective grief.

To see Graham before he began to speak was to wonder, however briefly, if his strength was equal to the task of delivering the message he had been asked to give. Any such thoughts faded quickly. The years seemed to fall away, and he spoke with a strength that belied his appearance. Amidst the grief that so many felt, Graham's message gave them, for a time, a place of grace, strength and hope. Acknowledging the horror of what had happened, and affirming that God is the God of all comfort, he told all those who were listening: 'We especially come together to confess our need of God. We have always needed God—from the very beginning of this nation; but now we need Him especially.' The mystery of evil and iniquity is a great mystery, Graham stated, but there is always a timeless truth to sustain us amidst such moments of questioning: God is 'a God of love and mercy and compassion in the midst of suffering.' The evangelist then told of a second lesson that he discerned. 'It's a lesson,' he said, 'about our need for each other.' He then shared vignettes of those who had risked their lives, and those who had lost their lives coming to the rescue of others.

September 11 was a day that reminded us all, with terrible swiftness, of the brevity of life. This thought formed a centerpiece of Graham's message: 'I doubt if even one of those people who got on those planes, or walked into the World Trade Center or the Pentagon that Tuesday morning, thought that this would be the last day of their lives. It didn't occur to them. And that's why each of us needs to face our own spiritual need and commit ourselves to God and his will now.'

Graham's closing words were words of hope:

'Here in this majestic National Cathedral we see all around us symbols of the Cross. For the Christian, the cross tells us that God understands our sin and our suffering, which He took upon Himself in the person of Jesus Christ. From the cross, God declares, "I love you. I know the heartaches and the sorrows and the pains that you feel. But I love you." The story does not end with the cross, for Easter points us beyond the tragedy of the cross to the empty tomb. It tells us that there is hope for eternal life, for Christ has conquered evil and death, and hell. Yes, there is hope!'

Graham's concluding words were both a capstone and a benediction:

'I've become an old man now, and I've preached all over the world. And the older I get the more I cling to that hope that I started with many years ago... My prayer today is that we will feel

Top: *The New York Times headlines for Wednesday 12th September 2001*
Above: *A poignient image of 9/11*

the loving arms of God wrapped around us, and will know in our hearts that He will never forsake us as we trust in Him.'

Millions mourned the sad and sober reason for Graham's message, but to hear that message and its affirmation of God's love, mercy and compassion in the midst of suffering was an unforgettable experience. As he slowly descended from the pulpit, many may have wondered if this was the last occasion they would

Washington's National Cathedral

The National Cathedral is a majestic place of worship. Its foundation stone was laid in 1907 and construction continued for another 83 years. When work was completed, a soaring edifice directly influenced by the great gothic cathedrals of Europe graced the summit of Mount St. Alban. The National Cathedral has been the site of many historic events. In 1968, Dr. Martin Luther King Jr. gave his last Sunday sermon from its Canterbury Pulpit. State funerals for three American presidents, Eisenhower, Ford and Reagan, have been held there. The National Cathedral is also home to two of America's premier schools: the St. Albans School (for boys), and the National Cathedral School for Girls, the Beauvoir School. Both institutions are part of the Protestant Episcopal Cathedral Foundation. St. Albans is situated in the shadow of the National Cathedral, on the fifty-seven-acre Cathedral Close in residential Northwest Washington. Known as America's 'national house of prayer,' the National Cathedral's website states that it is 'a spiritual resource for our nation: a great and beautiful edifice in the city of Washington, an indispensable ministry for people of all faiths and none, and a sacred place for our country in times of celebration, crisis, and sorrow.'

Above: The National Cathedral in Washington, one of America's most hallowed houses of worship
Below: The National Cathedral interior

hear him speak. Not a few were deeply grateful that he had been spared to give such a message.

A knighthood and degrees

Clearly, Billy Graham had entered the evening of his life. But while this was so, there remained more for him to do. Despite declining health, the onset of which had begun in the mid-1990s, he was able to conduct crusades on a more selective basis. Increasingly, the mantle of the BGEA was being passed to his son Franklin. On 7 November 1995 the BGEA board voted unanimously to install Franklin as vice-chair of the board, with direct succession to his father should he 'ever become incapacitated'. Meanwhile, as Graham entered the twilight years of his ministry, one moment of recognition took place. None could have been more special than this: an honor bestowed upon him by Queen Elizabeth II. On 5 December, 2001, Billy Graham was knighted in Washington by Sir Christopher Meyer, the British Ambassador, on behalf of the Queen. The award, said a British Foreign Office spokesperson, was bestowed in the light of Graham's 'huge and truly international contribution to civic and religious life over 60 years.' And so Billy Graham, a farmer's son from the American south, was made an Honorary Knight Commander of the Order of the British Empire, the knighthood bestowed on foreign nationals. Contrary to popular belief, those who receive this award do not use the title 'Sir,' but they are entitled to use the letters KBE after their name. Although it is well known that Billy Graham was awarded an honorary doctor of theology degree in 1981 from Debrecen Theological Academy in Hungary – incidentally the oldest Protestant theological seminary in the world founded in 1538 – it is not often appreciated just how many degrees he has been awarded in honour of his

Below: Billy Graham receiving his honorary knighthood

Above: Billy Graham's last crusade in New York City, held from 24–26 June 2005

outstanding achievements. No fewer than twenty-five doctoral degrees have been conferred on him from colleges in the United States and five other countries including South Korea and countries in Eastern Europe. Billy has always been in demand to address students at colleges across the world. Addressing the students at Jacksonville University, Florida in 1973 he encouraged them: 'To you who are graduating today, it's the beginning of a new stage in life. But what kind of world will you be facing?

Today we are putting our hopes in materialism, in technological progress, and in freedom from moral absolutes. They have all failed. They failed because they have been powerless to change the human heart. What is the answer? There is hope, if we will turn to God. Saint Augustine declared centuries ago, "You have created us for Yourself, O God, and our hearts are restless until they find rest in You."'

Another highpoint of ministry took place in June 2005. In what was said to be his last North American crusade, Graham and the BGEA team held a crusade at Flushing-Meadow's Corona Park in New York City. Words from one of his sermons during this crusade underscored the timelessness of the gospel message: 'Our world is constantly changing, but the needs of our hearts remain the same, and so does God's power to transform our lives and give us hope for the future.' These words are in many ways a summary of his message over the last sixty years.

Right:
Billy Graham and George Beverly Shea in the late 1990s, lifelong friends and ambassadors for Christ

However, there was yet another important event during which Graham would speak—a different kind of event. Over the course of one weekend in March 2006, he and his son Franklin led a 'Festival of Hope' in New Orleans, the city devastated by Hurricane Katrina. The festival was conceived as a gift to the people of New Orleans from the Samaritan's Purse (see page 104) and the BGEA. Pastors throughout New Orleans had requested help, and these two organizations responded, mobilizing thousands of Christians to aid in volunteer relief efforts and raising substantial sums of money to provide assistance. The Samaritan's Purse and the BGEA shouldered the entire cost of the festival of hope.

The homecall of Ruth

Within a year of the festival, health problems increased for both Billy and Ruth Graham. He had suffered from Parkinson's disease for over ten years, and experienced worrying bouts of fluid on the brain, pneumonia, broken hips and the onset of

---

Do converts last?

Early on, Billy Graham worried about this. But in ever-increasing numbers, wherever he went, he met converts active in ministry. Many suggest that converts do not last, but John Pollock notes that this is 'never sustained by…the evidence.' Stanley High, assigned by *Reader's Digest* to go to London a year after [Harringay 1954], found that 'a surprisingly large number of the converts are continuing.' Investigating more fully, he concluded that 'in every British or American city where a crusade had been held, [thousands] had become 'contagious Christians for whom life's most important business has become the spreading of that contagion. I have enough case histories…to fill…a book.'

In Canada in 1964, a 'learned gentleman' was asked about crusades like Billy Graham's. He said there was little lasting result. In thanking the speaker, R.A. Taylor, Director of the Church Army in Canada, commented 'I was delighted to be able to look down our table and ask those to please stand who were converts either at Toronto, 1955, or London. A good number of our students stood and were able to testify to the change in their lives which led them into full time service as a result of those campaigns.' Formal studies consistently confirm that large numbers of BGEA crusade converts continue in the faith, and that they 'touch every stratum of society and do so evenly.'

'But any assessment,' Pollock insists, must consider the many side effects of the crusades: 'a return to Biblical preaching, a new concern for religion among the world's press, the promotion of church unity, racial reconciliation and the strengthening of Christians in non-Christian lands—both by stimulating support and reinforcement from the West—and by the impact of crusades held in Asia, Africa and South America.'

Above: Billy and Ruth Graham at home in 1967 and 1993. Above their fireplace is the line from Martin Luther's hymn: 'A Mighty Fortress is Our God'

prostate cancer. Meanwhile, Ruth had suffered from a variety of illnesses for prolonged periods. In 1995 she was afflicted with spinal meningitis. Prior to this, she had endured many years of chronic back pain that had resulted from a fall in 1974 while testing a backyard swing for her grandchildren. With courage and fortitude, Ruth underwent several hip replacement procedures. Then, early in 2007, she became bedridden and contracted pneumonia. All the signs indicated that she might not live much longer. On June 10, Billy Graham released a statement through the BGEA: 'Ruth is my soul mate and best friend, and I cannot imagine living a single day without her by my side. I am more and more in love with her today than when we first met over 65 years ago as students at Wheaton College.'

Four days later, on 14 June 2007, Ruth Graham passed away, her husband and five children by her bedside. Shortly after, Billy Graham released this poignant tribute:

'My wife Ruth was the most incredible woman I have ever known. Whenever I was asked to name the finest Christian I ever met, I always replied, "My wife, Ruth." She was a spiritual giant, whose unparalleled knowledge of the Bible and commitment to prayer were a challenge and inspiration to everyone who knew her. My favorite photograph shows her sitting on our front porch at sunrise, quietly reading her Bible and sipping coffee—her daily routine for many years. A night never went by, when we were together, without us holding hands and praying before we went to sleep.'

One month prior to Ruth's death, the opening ceremonies for The Billy Graham Library were held in Charlotte, North Carolina. Yet while many dignitaries, including three former presidents, were there for the occasion, Billy's thoughts were for his wife. 'Today, I miss terribly my wife Ruth. I want to honor her and tell you how much I love her and tell you what a wonderful woman she has been. More than me, she deserves to be here today.' As for the Library itself, Graham had this to say: 'This building behind me is just a building. It's an instrument, a tool for the Gospel. The primary thing is the Gospel of Christ.'

On 7 November 2008 Billy Graham celebrated his 90th birthday. And while it was in many ways a festive occasion, with more than one hundred children, grandchildren, and great-grand-children in attendance, he took the opportunity to do something he had never done before: he used the Internet for the first time to send an email to a supporter of his ministry! Franklin Graham shared the story behind this unique way to mark a milestone: 'We helped him write it, but he pushed the button.' The younger Graham added that his father 'was asking me the other day, "How does it work?" And I said, "I don't know, but I know it does."'

Flashes of humor also set this special occasion apart. Graham's body had grown frail, but his mind remained sharp. He had one birthday wish: to turn 91. In an interview with *Christianity Today*, his son Franklin noted: 'George Beverly Shea turns 100 in February, so I think Daddy's trying to catch up to him…I try to tell him from time to time, "Dad, let's go for a walk," and he will look at me a little bit disgusted and say, "You wait until you turn 90."'

Now, in the evening of his life, Graham had established a modest routine that lends a

Above: *Ruth Graham, 'the most incredible woman' beloved wife and faithful follower of Christ*

gentle rhythm to his days: 'He wakes up early to a cup of coffee before going back to bed to rest more. He eats something simple for lunch, like a peanut butter and jelly sandwich. He stays engaged with current events as he watches television news, reads newspaper headlines, and asks the staff to read stories aloud. Franklin Graham offers: 'Right now we just want to get around him and love him, have a meal together, share some laughs and memories… Of course, he misses my mother, and he knows he's not going to be on this earth much longer. He's looking forward to the time when he can not only be reunited with his wife but also stand in the presence of the Lord Jesus Christ, whom he has served all his life.'

Characteristically, Graham himself has said that he thought often about what those first moments in Glory will be like. 'I have often said that the first thing I am going to do when I get to Heaven is to ask, "Why

The Billy Graham Library

Under a hot North Carolina sun in May 2007 three former presidents, Jimmy Carter, George H W Bush and Bill Clinton, joined the assembled guests at the opening ceremonies for The Billy Graham Library in Charlotte, North Carolina. It was a singular event, and one which underscored the unique place an evangelist from humble beginnings had come to hold in America's national life. All three presidents spoke on the occasion, expressing gratitude for the spiritual guidance and friendship Graham extended to them. Later, when Graham himself spoke, *Time* magazine reported that he stole the show: 'I feel like I've been attending my own funeral,' he said—a quip that showed both his sense of humor and a sense of humility that has grown with the years.

The Library facility, modeled after the dairy farm where Graham spent his youth, features A Journey of Faith, 'a presentation that offers multimedia displays and re-creations of historic moments in Billy Graham's life and ministry. Spanning the decades from the 1940s to the present, the exhibits show how God prepared and used this humble man to take the message of His unchanging love to an ever-changing world.'

Visitors to The Billy Graham Library may tour the restored Graham family homeplace, enjoy contemplative moments in the adjacent Prayer Garden, and learn about Ruth Graham's life and work with her husband in a special room dedicated to her.

Above: The Billy Graham Library, modelled after the dairy farm of his youth

me, Lord? Why did you choose a farmboy from North Carolina to preach to so many people, to have such a wonderful team of associates, and to have a part in what You were doing in the latter half of the twentieth century? I have thought about that question a great deal, but I know also that only God knows the answer.'

Perhaps Russ Busby, the official photographer of BGEA, has answered the question with profound simplicity: 'I believe the only way to explain Billy's success is simply that God chose Billy Graham to represent him at this particular time in history.'

TRAVEL INFORMATION

The National Cathedral

Massachusetts and Wisconsin Avenues, NW
Washington, DC
20016–5098
Website (including travel directions) www.nationalcathedral.org
The website for the National Cathedral details a number of activities held year round relating to music and the arts. The site states: 'In addition to our own highly regarded choirs and liturgical music, you can enjoy concerts and recitals by visiting musicians in one of the nation's most magnificent settings. The Cathedral is also home to a fascinating display of craftsmanship and the visual arts, from stone carving to floral arrangements to special exhibits.'

The National Cathedral website also states that it offers an array of Cathedral lectures and educational programs. These 'reflect an intellectually probing, generous-spirited Christianity, rooted in the Episcopal tradition yet open and welcoming to people of all faiths and perspectives. Uplift your spirit, engage your mind, and deepen your understanding of today's world.'

The Billy Graham Library

www.billygraham.org/bglibrary
Opening hours:
9.30–5pm closed on on Sunday. Admission is free.

My hope for you

If you and I could sit together for a few minutes to talk about the future, I would very much want to share with you the following thought. The Bible has much to say about the brevity of life and the necessity of preparing for eternity. I am convinced that only when a man is prepared to die is he also prepared to live. If you want to know what God is like then take a look at Jesus Christ. To His disciples Jesus said, 'I am the way and the truth and the life. No one comes to the Father except through me' (John 14:6). Surrender your life to the Lord Jesus Christ. Let Him come into your heart and change you. He can give you a new dimension of living. He will help you achieve your goals as you seek His guidance. God knows what is best for us. The Bible says, 'Whoever believes in the Son has eternal life' (John 3:36). I pray that you will make this important decision today.

Billy Graham Training Center at The Cove

Be anxious for nothing; but in everything by prayer and supplication, with thanksgiving, let your requests be made known unto God. And the peace of God, which passeth all understanding, shall keep your hearts and minds through Christ Jesus. *Philippians 4:6-7 (KJV)*

Timeline for Billy Graham's life

1918 **7 November.** Billy Graham is born in a frame farmhouse outside Charlotte, North Carolina.

1934 **30 Aug. to 25 Nov.** BG is converted during a series of revival meetings led by Mordecai Ham.

1943 **14 June.** BG graduates from Wheaton College in Illinois, and soon after is called as pastor of the Western Springs Baptist Church, in Western Spring, Illinois.

1943 **13 August.** BG marries Ruth McCue Bell in Montreat, North Carolina.

1944 **January.** BG becomes main speaker of the popular radio program *Songs in the Night* on station WCFL in Chicago, Illinois.

1944 **October.** BG begins working almost fulltime with Youth for Christ (YFC), although officially remains pastor of the Village Church (formerly of the Western Springs Baptist Church) until the fall of 1945.

1946 **18 March to 28 April.** BG and his ministry team conduct a YFC tour of Great Britain and Europe.

1947 **December.** BG becomes president of Northwestern Schools in Minneapolis, Minnesota.

1949 **25 Sept. to 20 Nov.** The Christ for Greater Los Angeles Crusade, after which BG becomes America's most prominent evangelist.

1950 **8 April.** BG visits D L Moody's grave, a moment of great symbolism and inspiration for his ministry.

1950 **17 Sept.** Incorporation of the Billy Graham Evangelistic Association (BGEA).

1952 **25 Feb.** BG resigns as president of Northwestern Schools.

1953 **20 Jan.** Attends first inauguration of President Dwight D. Eisenhower.

1954 **March to 22 May.** The Greater London, or Harringay Crusade.

1954 **25 May.** Meeting with Prime Minister Winston Churchill in London, England.

1955 **22 May.** Preaches before Queen Elizabeth II of the United Kingdom.

1956 **17 Jan. to 13 Feb.** BG and the BGEA team undertake an evangelistic tour of India.

1956 **13 Nov.** BG visits Wheaton College and receives honorary Doctor of Letters degree.

1957 **11 May.** BG arrives in New York City for start of the NYC Crusade, and is interviewed by Walter Cronkite on the CBS Evening News—a major nationwide telecast.

1957 **15 May to 1 Sept.** BG and the BGEA team conduct NYC Crusade.

1957 **18 July.** Martin Luther King, Jr. leads assembled congregants in prayer at the NYC Crusade—a major step forward in racial integration.

1959 **15 Feb. to 31 May.** The Southern Cross Crusade throughout Australia and New Zealand.

1960 **12 Jan. to 13 Mar.** BG and the BGEA conduct an African evangelistic tour.

1960 **August.** BG and BGEA hold a series of crusades in Switzerland. BG meets with eminent theologians Karl Barth and Emil Brunner during this period.

1961 **12 December.** BG meets with president-elect John F. Kennedy in Washington, D.C.

- **1962 28 May (?).** On the eve of the Greater Chicago Crusade, BG meets again with Martin Luther King, Jr.
- **1962 30 May to 17 June.** Greater Chicago Crusade.
- **1964 18–19 Feb.** BG speaks at Harvard Divinity School in Cambridge, Massachusetts.
- **1965 29 Nov.** President Lyndon Johnson attends BG crusade service in Houston, Texas.
- **1966 1 June to 2 July.** BG and the BGEA team hold Greater London Crusade.
- **1966 26 Oct. to 4 Nov.** BG attends World Congress on Evangelism in Berlin, Germany.
- **1968 19 April to 28 April.** BG and BGEA team hold Sydney Crusade in Sydney, Australia.
- **1968 8 June.** BG attends Robert Kennedy's funeral.
- **1969 28 March (?).** Meeting with Israeli Prime Minister Golda Meir in Israel.
- **1972 19 Nov.** BG meets with Mother Teresa.
- **1972 23 Nov.** BG meets with Indian Prime Minister Indira Gandhi.
- **1974 16 July to 25 July.** BG takes leading part in the International Congress on World Evangelization in Lausanne, Switzerland.
- **1974 8 Dec.** BG meets with Alexandr Solzhenitsyn.
- **1980 30 Jan. to 16 Feb.** BG and BGEA team hold Oxford and Cambridge University Missions.
- **1981 12 Jan.** BG meets with Pope John Paul II in the Vatican.
- **1982 7 May through 13 May.** BG visits the Soviet Union and holds key series of meeting with Christians there.
- **1983 23 Feb.** BG receives Presidential Medal of Freedom from President Ronald Reagan.
- **1984 May to July.** During this period, BG and the BGEA team take part in the Mission England evangelistic outreach.
- **1989 31 May.** BG meets with Prime Minister Margaret Thatcher. The next day BG meets with President George H.W. Bush.
- **1989 21 Jun. to 2 July.** BG and the BGEA team take part in the Mission '89 evangelism outreach.
- **1991 10 July (?).** BG meets with USSR President Mikhail Gorbachev.
- **1991 13 July.** BG meets with Russian President Boris Yeltsin.
- **1995 8 Nov.** BG announces on his 77th birthday that his son Franklin had been elected by the BGEA board as vice chairman of the board and will become the head of the BGEA when Billy Graham dies or is incapacitated.
- **1996 2 May.** Billy and Ruth Graham are awarded the Congressional Gold Medal.
- **2000 5 Nov.** BG meets with president-elect and Mrs. George W. Bush.
- **2001 14 Sept.** BG preaches at the service held in the National Cathedral in Washington, D.C. on the National day of Prayer and Remembrance held in response to the terrorist attacks in New York and Washington on September 11.
- **2005 24 Jun. to 26 Jun.** BG and the BGEA team hold Greater New York Crusade.
- **2007 5 June.** Public opening of the Billy Graham Library in Charlotte, North Carolina.
- **2007 14 June.** The death of BG's beloved wife Ruth Bell Graham.
- **2008 8 Nov.** BG celebrates his ninetieth birthday.

Books by Billy Graham (in order of publication)

Calling Youth to Christ (1947).
America's Hour of Decision (1951).
I Saw Your Sons at War (1953).
Peace with God (1953, 1984).
Freedom from the Seven Deadly Sins (1955).
The Secret of Happiness (1955, 1985).
Billy Graham Talks to Teenagers (1958).
My Answer (1960).
Billy Graham Answers Your Questions (1960).
World Aflame (1965).
The Challenge (1969).
The Jesus Generation (1971).
Angels: God's Secret Agents (1975, 1985).
How to be Born Again (1977).
The Holy Spirit (1978).
Till Armageddon (1981).
Approaching Hoofbeats (1983).
A Biblical Standard for Evangelists (1984).
Unto the Hills (1986).
Facing Death and the Life After (1987).
Answers to Life's Problems (1988).
Hope for the Troubled Heart (1991).
Storm Warning (1992).
Just As I Am (1997).
Hope for Each Day (2002).
The Key to Personal Peace (2003).
Living in God's Love: The New York Crusade (2005)
The Journey: How to Live by Faith in an Uncertain World (2006)

Above: *Billy Graham in 1972, preacher of the gospel, faithful servant of Christ*

Further reading

Billy Graham, *Just As I Am: The Autobiography of Billy Graham*, (San Francisco: HarperOne, 2007). Tenth anniversary edition.
John Pollock, *Billy Graham: The Authorised Biography*, (London: Hodder and Stoughton, 1966.)
John Pollock, *The Billy Graham Story*, (Grand Rapids, Michigan: Zondervan, 2003).
Russ Busby, *Billy Graham—God's Ambassador* (BGEA Tehabi Books 1999). Biographical information archived at the website for the Billy Graham Evangelistic Association: www.billygraham.org.
Also the Billy Graham Center's 'Select Chronology Listing of Events in the History of the Billy Graham Evangelistic Association.'
Of additional interest is: Harold Myra and Marshall Shelley, *The Leadership Secrets of Billy Graham*, (Zondervan, 2005).
William Martin, *A Prophet with Honor: The Billy Graham Story*, (Harper Perennial, 1992).

Acknowledgments

First and foremost I owe a tremendous debt to John Akers, the editorial coordinator for Billy Graham's autobiography, *Just As I Am*. In particular, I am deeply grateful for a lengthy phone visit with Dr. Akers in the spring of 2008, during which he very kindly offered to send me the latest edition of *Just As I Am,* along with a copy of *Billy Graham: God's Ambassador*—the most comprehensive pictorial biography of Dr. Graham published to date. For the use of many pictures from this book I am indebted to Russ Busby. Dr. Akers also expressed his willingness to review this book in draft form, in order to ensure accuracy and correct any inadvertent errors in the text. These courtesies are a mark of signal kindness that I will always remember. The same is true of John Pollock, a treasured friend, and as fine a Christian gentleman as I have ever known. He graciously granted permission for me to quote as needed from his various biographies of Billy Graham. I wish to acknowledge here as well the deep gratitude I feel for an autographed copy of John's book *The Billy Graham Story,* (Grand Rapids, Michigan: Zondervan, 2003).

For the use of several beautiful photographs of the Wheaton College campus, I wish to thank Ellen Rising Morris, Vince Morris and the administration at Wheaton. Ellen's images have added an artist's touch to this book, and I feel privileged to use them.

I am grateful as well to Dennis Robson, who very generously allowed me to quote from his recollections of serving as Billy and Ruth Graham car driver during the Earl's Court Crusade of 1966. To my knowledge, these recollections have never appeared in print. I feel thus doubly honored to make use of them.

Brian Edwards is a cherished friend and gifted editor, whose counsel I value very highly indeed. I also wish to thank Wayne McMaster for bringing his talents in graphic design and layout to bear on this book. It is a distinct pleasure to collaborate with both men and benefit from their expertise.

About the Author

Kevin Belmonte is an award-winning author who resides in a seaside village in New England. Of British ancestry, his is a literary family that includes the poets Robert Frost and Henry Wadsworth Longfellow. On several occasions, Kevin has served as a script consultant for the BBC. He has done so as well for PBS—the BBC's American counterpart. For six years, he was the lead historical consultant for the acclaimed motion picture Amazing Grace. Kevin is also the author of two biographies of William Wilberforce including, in this series, Travel with William Wilberforce—the friend of humanity. He and his wife Kelly are the proud parents of their young son, Sam.

Day One Audio Books

If you would like to download this Billy Graham Travel Guide as an audio book please go to www.dayone.co.uk and click on Audio Books. Also available as an audio book: Travel with William Tyndale and Travel with John Calvin.

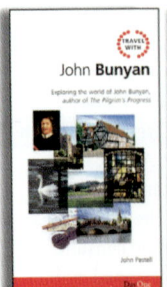

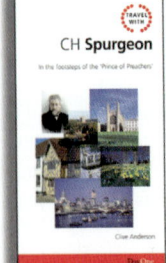

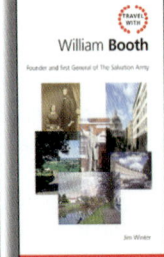

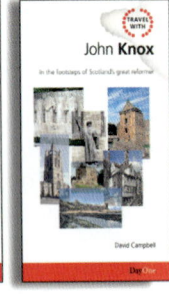

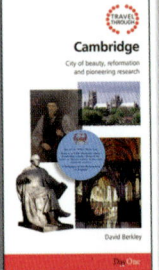

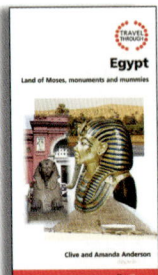

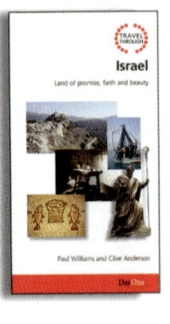

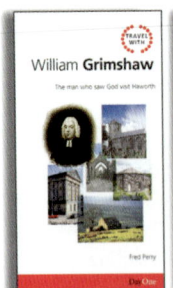

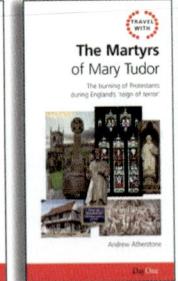

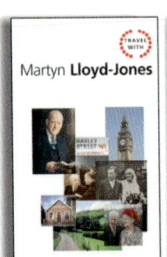

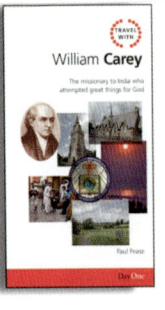

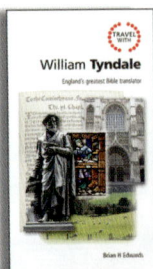

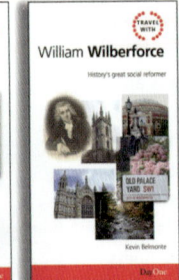

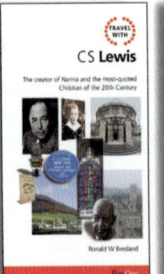

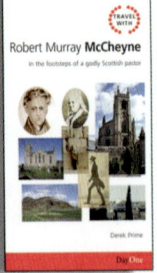

Travel With series

- **John Bunyan** — Exploring the world of John Bunyan, author of The Pilgrim's Progress — John Pestell
- **CH Spurgeon** — In the footsteps of the 'Prince of Preachers' — Clive Anderson
- **William Booth** — Founder and first General of The Salvation Army — Jim Winter
- **John Knox** — In the footsteps of Scotland's great reformer — David Campbell
- **Through The British Museum with the Bible** — Brian Edwards, Clive Anderson
- **Cambridge** — City of beauty, reformation and pioneering research — David Berkley
- **Egypt** — Land of Moses, monuments and mummies — Clive and Amanda Anderson
- **Israel** — Land of promise, faith and beauty — Paul Williams and Clive Anderson
- **William Grimshaw** — The man who saw God visit Haworth — Fred Perry
- **The Martyrs of Mary Tudor** — The burning of Protestants during England's 'reign of terror' — Andrew Atherstone
- **Martyn Lloyd-Jones** — Philip Eveson
- **William Carey** — The missionary to India who attempted great things for God — Paul Pease
- **William Tyndale** — England's greatest Bible translator — Brian H Edwards
- **William Wilberforce** — History's great social reformer — Kevin Belmonte
- **CS Lewis** — The creator of Narnia and the most-quoted Christian of the 20th Century — Ronald W Bresland
- **Robert Murray McCheyne** — In the footsteps of a godly Scottish pastor — Derek Prime

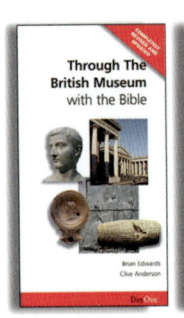

Day One

ALSO AVAILABLE

Oxford: City of saints, scholars and dreaming spires

For many centuries, the city of Oxford has played a central part in England's national and religious life. Home to one of the world's oldest universities, it has trained a glittering array of leaders and opinion-formers: kings, prime ministers, archbishops, scientists, soldiers, theologians, poets, and explorers. This book tells the lively account of Oxford's impact upon the history of England, especially its Christian history, from the earliest times to the present day. Along the way we meet medieval friars, outspoken reformers, martyred bishops, puritans and radicals, revivalists and secularists, scholars and missionaries.

ORDER TODAY

USA - CALL DAYONE PUBLICATIONS ON 📞 706 554 5907
UK - CALL DAYONE PUBLICATIONS ON 📞 01568 613740

DAY ONE TRAVEL GUIDES

The Day One Travel Guide series introduces our Christian heritage through people and places that have been influential in the history of western civilization and far beyond. They introduce the lives of great Christian leaders, past and present, and tour lands and cities with a strong biblical connection. They are written by authors who are specialists in their subject. Attractively produced with around 150 informative drawings and photographs. A tour guide to introduce the places associated with the subject. Equally valuable for the armchair traveler they bring people and places alive.

- **PLACES OF INTEREST**
- **PACKED WITH COLOUR PHOTOS**
- **CLEAR ILLUSTRATED MAPS**
- **GREAT GIFT IDEA**
- **128 PAGES**

FOOTSTEPS OF THE PAST

A series of children's activity books twinned with the Travel Guides

ROMANS, GLADIATORS AND GAMES
In the British Museum, explore the Roman world of the first Christians

KINGS, PHARAOHS AND BANDITS
In the British Museum, explore the world of Abraham to Esther

WILLIAM TYNDALE
He was threatened, hunted, betrayed and killed so that we could have the Bible in English

JOHN BUNYAN
How a hooligan and soldier became a preacher, prisoner and famous writer

WILLIAM CAREY
The story of a country boy and shoe mender whose big dreams took him to India

WILLIAM BOOTH
The troublesome teenager who changed the lives of people no one else would touch

WILLIAM WILBERFORCE
The millionaire child who worked so hard to win the freedom of African slaves

C S LEWIS
The story of one of the world's most famous authors who sold over a hundred million books

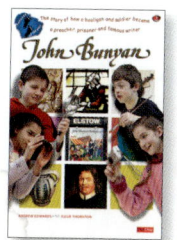

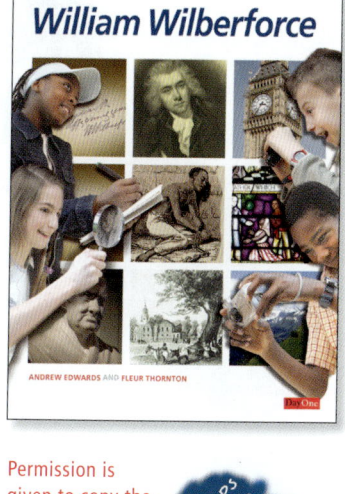

Permission is given to copy the activity pages and associated text for use as class or group material

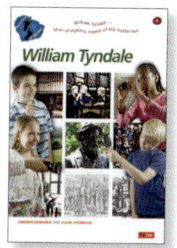

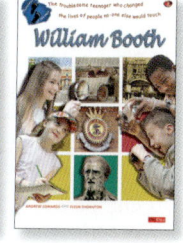

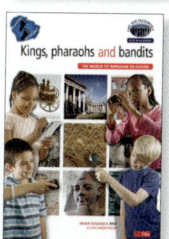

CENTRES OF BILLY GRAHAM'S PREACHING IN THE UK

1. **Aberdeen** 1946, 47, 55, 91
2. **Belfast** 1946, 47, 61
3. **Birmingham** 1946, 47, 84
4. **Blackheath (London)** 1946
5. **Blackpool** 1982
6. **Bournemouth** 1946
7. **Bradford** 1947
8. **Bristol** 1946, 84
9. **Cambridge** 1955, 80
10. **Chatham** 1947
11. **Cardiff** 1946
12. **Derby** 1969
13. **Dudley** 1946
14. **Dundee** 1946
15. **Eastbourne (first)** 1946, 47
16. **Edinburgh** 1946, 55, 91
17. **Falkirk** 1969
18. **Glasgow** 1947, 55, 61, 91
19. **Gorseinon** 1946
20. **Hull** 1946, 69
21. **Inverness** 1955
22. **Ipswich** 1984
23. **Kewick** 1975
24. **Lewisham (London)** 1947
25. **Liverpool** 1946, 84
26. **London** 1946, 47, 48, 54, 55, 59, 61, 66, 67, 69, 70 89
27. **Manchester** 1946, 48, 61
28. **Newcastle-upon-Tyne** 1946
29. **Norwich** 1984
30. **Oldham** 1947
31. **Oxford** 1955, 80
32. **Pontypridd** 1946
33. **Reading** 1947
34. **Sandringham** 1984
35. **Sheffield** 1985
36. **Stockton on Tees** 1946
37. **Southampton** 1946
38. **Sunderland** 1984
39. **Swansea** 1946, 61
40. **York** 1946